THE
OCCULT
BOOK

THE
OCCULT
BOOK

A CHRONOLOGICAL JOURNEY
from ALCHEMY *to* WICCA

JOHN MICHAEL GREER

STERLING
New York

STERLING
New York

An Imprint of Sterling Publishing Co., Inc.
1166 Avenue of the Americas
New York, NY 10036

ISBN 978-1-4549-2577-4

Distributed in Canada by Sterling Publishing Co., Inc.
c/o Canadian Manda Group, 664 Annette Street
Toronto, Ontario, M6S 2C8, Canada
Distributed in the United Kingdom by GMC Distribution Services
Castle Place, 166 High Street, Lewes, East Sussex, BN7 1XU, England
Distributed in Australia by NewSouth Books
45 Beach Street, Coogee, NSW 2034, Australia

For information about custom editions, special sales, and premium and corporate purchases,
please contact Sterling Special Sales at 800–805–5489 or specialsales@sterlingpublishing.com.

Manufactured in China

6 8 10 9 7

sterlingpublishing.com

Cover and Endpaper Design by Spencer Charles
For Image Credits, see page 211

"The world is not prepared yet to understand the philosophy of Occult Sciences—
let them assure themselves first of all that there are beings in an invisible
world, whether 'Spirits' of the dead or Elementals; and that there are hidden
powers in man, which are capable of making a God of him on earth."

—H. P. Blavatsky (1831–1891)

CONTENTS

INTRODUCTION

"The gates of the Mysteries stand ever ajar, and those who will may
pass through into the spacious domicile of spirit."

—Manly P. Hall, *The Secret Teachings of All Ages*

IN MOST OF THE WORLD'S CULTURES AND through most of the world's history, the things that people in the modern Western world consider "occult"—amulets and talismans, omens and divinations, spells and charms, spirits good and evil—are simply part of everyday life. If you go to a Shinto shrine in Japan, for example, or to a temple of one of the traditional religions of West Africa, you can count on seeing things done there that would qualify as occultism in Europe or America. In these societies, nothing sets those things apart from any other body of traditional knowledge. People engage in them all the time without ever suspecting that they are doing something secret, forbidden, or irrational.

In the Western world, for complicated historical reasons, this hasn't been the case. Instead, starting in Roman times and accelerating with the triumph of Christianity, what we know as "the occult" was set apart as forbidden lore. From the first stirrings of antioccult hysteria through the horrors of the Burning Times, when hundreds of thousands of people were tortured and executed on suspicion of practicing magic, tremendous social pressures backed by the threat of violence fell on anyone who took an interest in the occult— yet the occult traditions of the Western world

managed to survive all that, finding new practitioners in every generation. That astonishing story of suppression, survival, and rebirth extending over more than two and a half millennia is the subject of this book.

The word *occult* literally means "hidden," and its application to what we now call the occult has a long history. During the Renaissance, writers who wanted to refer to magic, divination, and the alternative spirituality connected with them began to use the term *occult philosophy*—that is, "hidden philosophy"—for those subjects. That habit became permanent when Cornelius Agrippa titled his great textbook of Renaissance magic *Three Books of Occult Philosophy*. Later, during the revival of magic in the nineteenth century, French authors started using the word *occultisme*—in English, *occultism*—for the same subjects.

It can be useful to think of occultism as the rejected knowledge of the Western world. Every society has some body of knowledge that has been condemned by the intellectual authorities of the time but still is studied and taught outside the normal channels of education and public opinion. In industrial nations today, the explosive growth of knowledge has been matched by an equally explosive growth in rejected knowledge, and much of this has nothing to do with occultism. Still, the occult remains the oldest and the most savagely persecuted of all the Western world's bodies of rejected knowledge.

Among the core elements of occultism are these:

Magic—"the science and art of causing changes in consciousness at will," according to its great twentieth-century practitioner Dion Fortune. The mage, or practitioner of magic, uses rituals, symbolism, meditation, and other methods to enter into unusual states of consciousness in which, according to occult teachings, subtle powers can be directed and disembodied entities contacted to cause changes in the world.

Patent medicine label, c. 1892, depicting a witch at her cauldron.

Divination—more commonly known as fortune-telling, this is the art of knowing hidden things in the present and the secrets of the future through the same subtle links that in occult tradition make magic work. The Tarot card reader who shuffles and deals cards, the astrologer who studies the positions of the planets at a particular moment, and diviners using other methods all try to tap into the flow of unseen forces that will allow them to glimpse the unknown.

Initiation—the process by which an ordinary person develops the powers and abilities needed to master magic and divination. There are many methods of initiation, but the most famous are elaborate ceremonies that enact symbolic dramas, catalyzing changes in the consciousness of the new initiate. The mystery rituals of ancient Greece were famous initiations in their time; more recently, the rituals of magical lodges such as the Hermetic Order of the Golden Dawn and the Martinist Order serve the same function.

Alchemy—often dismissed by modern scientists as a failed attempt to turn lead into gold, alchemy is far more diverse—and far more practical. To an alchemist, every material substance has a potential for perfection, and the methods of alchemy are used to help each substance achieve its perfection. Alchemists thus prepare herbal medicines, practice spiritual meditation, and work with a dizzying array of substances in their pursuit of hidden knowledge.

Occult philosophy—underlying these occult practices is a philosophy that explains how and why occultism works. Three main schools of occult philosophy have played a predominant role in the history of occultism. Neoplatonism, an offshoot of the philosophy of Plato, emerged in ancient Greece; Hermeticism, a blend of Greek philosophy and Egyptian magical teaching, had its start

66 Magic is the traditional science of the secrets of nature, which has come down to us from the mages. 99

–Éliphas Lévi, *Doctrine and Ritual of High Magic,* 1855

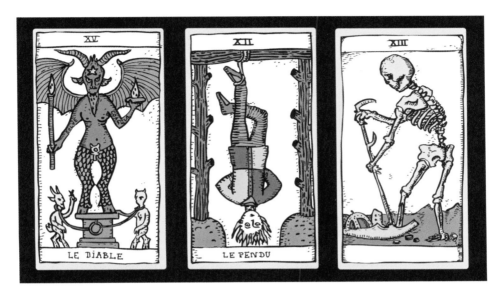

Tarot-card reading is an example of divination, or fortune-telling, one of the main elements of occultism.

in Egypt; and Cabala (also spelled Kabbalah and Qabalah), the most recent of the three, was born in the Jewish communities of southern France. All three have strong similarities with one another and draw on many of the same sources.

These core ingredients, combined with one another and with an assortment of other practices and teachings, make up the heart of the occult traditions of the West. From the sixth century BCE, when the first known occult school was founded in the Western world by Pythagoras of Samos, they have been handed down—sometimes publicly and sometimes in secret, sometimes by way of organizations such as the Rosicrucians and sometimes from individual teachers to students—all the way to the present.

The pages that follow present a hundred important events in the history of occultism: stations, if you will, along the road that leads from Pythagoras to the present day. It is a long and winding journey that covers the whole range of human possibility from the heights of spiritual aspiration to the depths of folly and fraud, and an uncomfortably long part of the route is made hideous by the screams of the tortured and the scent of burning flesh.

Where will the road lead next as the occult traditions of today respond to the challenges of tomorrow? No one knows, but the transformations through which occultism already has passed suggest that its story is far from over.

PYTHAGORAS COMES TO CROTONA

THE GREEK COLONIAL CITY OF CROTONA IN southern Italy was a thriving metropolis in the sixth century BCE and attracted immigrants from every part of the bustling Greek world. None of them would become as famous as a middle-aged man who came there some time in the second half of that century. His name was Pythagoras (c. 570 BCE–c. 495 BCE), and his arrival in Crotona marks the dawn of the history of occultism in the Western world.

Born in Samos, off the coast of what is now Turkey, Pythagoras left his homeland in search of knowledge, studying with the philosophers Thales of Miletus and Pherecydes of Syros. Unsatisfied with their instruction, he set sail for Egypt, where he studied with the priests of Thebes for a time, and then traveled to Babylon to learn what the astrologer-priests of that land had to teach. Finally he returned to the Greek world and was initiated into mystery cults in Greece and Crete before finally settling in Crotona.

There he set up an order, the Pythagorean Brotherhood, to pass on the teachings he had learned in his journeys. Those who joined the school lived under a vow of silence for the first five years and only then were admitted into the inner teachings of the order. Little is known about those teachings, but they certainly included belief in reincarnation, the meaning of numbers and geometry, and rules governing everyday life.

Late in the sixth century, the Pythagorean Brotherhood intervened in Crotona's politics, supporting the aristocratic party against the democratic party. When the aristocrats lost, a mob burned down the headquarters of the brotherhood. Survivors of the brotherhood scattered throughout the Greek world, carrying Pythagoras's teachings with them. From them and their students, the traditions of Western occultism ultimately descend.

SEE ALSO: Death of Plato (347 BCE), Apollonius of Tyana (1st Century CE), Gerard Thibault's *Academy of the Sword* (1630)

Pythagoras, depicted here in this seventeenth-century etching, believed in sacred geometry and the "transmigration of the soul," or reincarnation.

EMPEDOCLES INVENTS THE FOUR ELEMENTS

THE MATHEMATICAL MYSTICISM OF Pythagoras, hugely influential though it went on to be, found few takers in the busy world of ancient Greek philosophy. Most thinkers of that time argued that behind the world we experience there had to be a single source from which everything else came into being—and most of them argued that that source had to be a material substance. Thales of Miletus, the first Greek philosopher, argued that the source was water; Heraclitus thought that it was fire; and others had different opinions.

Empedocles (c. 495 BCE–c. 432 BCE), the man who would combine those beliefs into an enduring synthesis, was born in the Greek colonial city of Akragas in Sicily. He took an active part in the rough-and-tumble politics of his hometown, was exiled to Greece, and supposedly committed suicide by flinging himself into the crater of the volcano Vesuvius. At some point in his busy life, he found time to write two long poems: *Purifications*, on religion, and *On Nature*, the first statement of the theory of the four elements.

To Empedocles, the sheer diversity of the world showed that there could be no single source of everything. Instead, he argued, four basic substances—fire, air, water, and earth—made up all things by combining and separating. Empedocles was on to something; when scientists today describe the world as being made up of solids, liquids, gases, and energy, they're using Empedocles's classification under other names.

It was in the emerging traditions of Western occultism that Empedocles's theory would find its lasting home. The habit of dividing the world into the four categories of fiery, airy, watery, and earthy things proved so useful to mages, diviners, and other occultists that the four elements became far and away the most influential set of symbols in occult theory and practice.

SEE ALSO: Death of Plato (347 BCE)

A figure of Empedocles, by artist Friedrich Beer (1846–1912), at the Museum of Natural History, Vienna. Empedocles is best known for his theory that all matter is composed of four elements: fire, air, water, and earth.

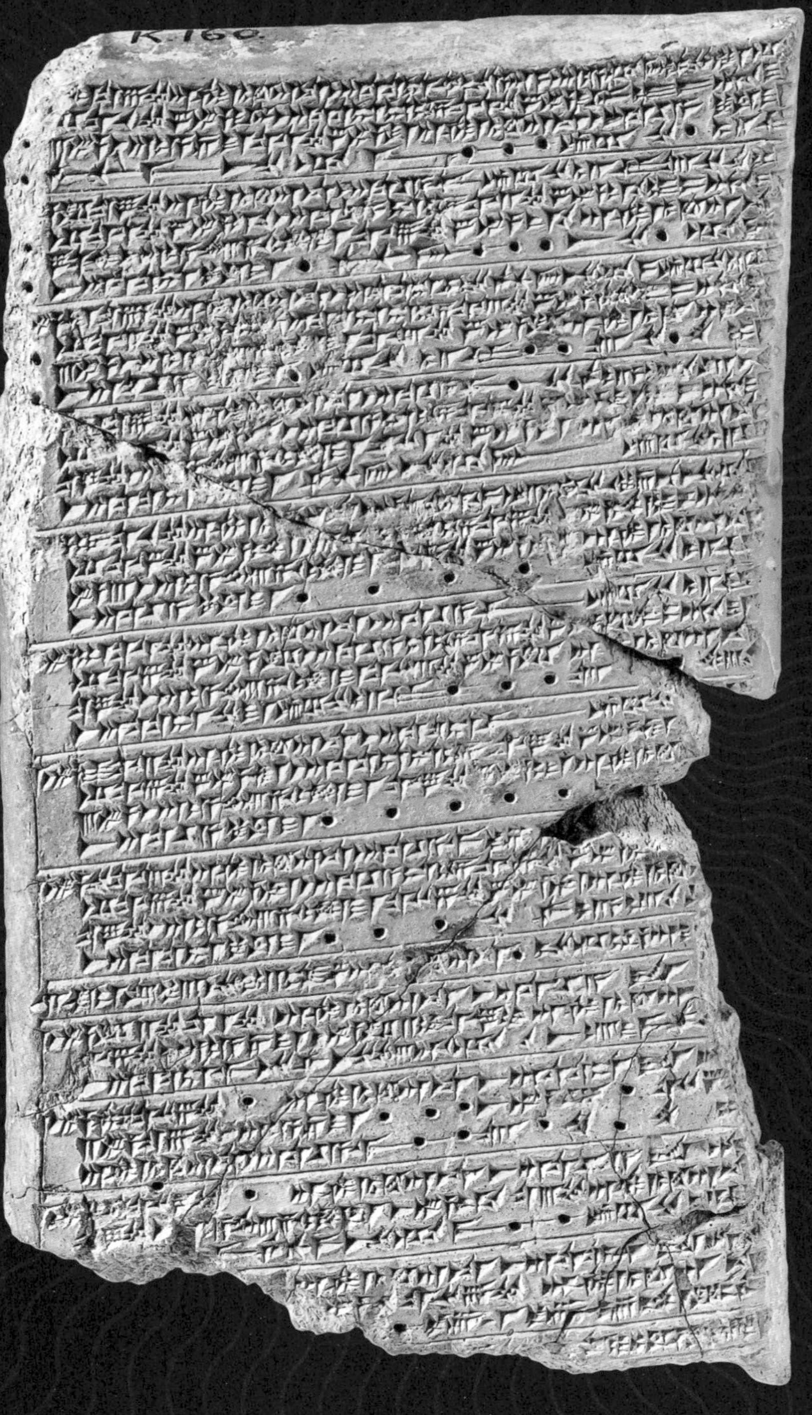
K.160

THE FIRST HOROSCOPES

FOR MANY CENTURIES, THE PRIESTS AND priestesses of Mesopotamia—the "land between the rivers" in what is now Iraq and southeastern Turkey—watched the heavens and recorded what they saw on baked clay tablets, hoping to tease out from the movements of the sky the inscrutable will of their gods. The Mesopotamian tradition of astrology dates back very far; the oldest surviving record of that tradition, the Venus tablet of Ammisaduqa, dates from some time around 1650 BCE and shows a mastery of star lore that must have taken many centuries to gain.

To the star watchers of the ancient Middle East, though, it was not just the positions of the sun, moon, and planets that mattered; clouds and other aerial phenomena also had their place in the clay tablet records. Furthermore, scholars of that time believed that the heavens warned of the rise and fall of kingdoms, not the destinies of individuals. It was only later, when the priests and priestesses began to study the heavens at the time when the son or daughter of a king was born, that the first steps were taken toward astrology as we know it.

By the seventh century BCE, entire libraries were devoted to records of what had happened under this or that set of celestial circumstances and rules for interpreting the sky had become standardized. It was not until the latter part of the fifth century BCE, though, that astrologers in Mesopotamia began applying those rules to the birth data of individuals and casting horoscopes in the modern sense of the word.

That was the point astrology had reached when the armies of Alexander the Great conquered Mesopotamia. In the wake of the conquest, wisdom traditions across the ancient world mixed and mingled, and astrology spread throughout the Mediterranean world.

SEE ALSO: Translation of *Picatrix* (1256), John Dee Schedules a Royal Coronation (1559), Casting Spells for the Pope (1628), William Lilly's *Christian Astrology* (1647), Evangeline Adams Acquitted of Fortune-Telling (1914), Dane Rudhyar's *The Astrology of Personality* (1936)

The Venus tablet of Ammisaduqa, c. 1650 BCE, is the oldest surviving record of Mesopotamian astrology.

DEATH OF PLATO

HIS REAL NAME WAS ARISTOCLES OF Athens, but everyone called him Plato because of his very broad shoulders. A famous wrestler in his youth, Plato (c. 428 BCE–347 BCE) took up philosophy at the age of twenty and became the foremost disciple of Socrates. When his teacher was executed by the Athenian government in 399 BCE, Plato left his hometown for Megara, where he studied geometry with the famous mathematician Euclid. Thereafter he traveled around the Mediterranean world as Pythagoras had, studying wisdom wherever he could and getting into and out of an assortment of scrapes. Finally he returned to Athens and founded a school, the Academy, which survived long after his death.

Plato's philosophy was strongly influenced by the teachings of Pythagoras and Empedocles. He taught that beyond the world known by our five senses—the world of Becoming—lay the world of Being. Everything we experience in the world of Becoming is a reflection of eternal patterns that exist in the world of Being, and the task of the true philosopher is to get past the misleading data provided by the senses and know the world of Being directly with the mind.

There was no trace of occultism in Plato's published dialogues and only a few hints concerning unwritten teachings in a few letters attributed to him. None of this kept occultists from adopting Platonic philosophy as a guiding theory for their work—and this they did across the ancient Greek world. After his death, as a bitter time of troubles settled over the Greek lands, more and more intellectuals turned away from the rationalist philosophies that had done so little to keep their societies on an even keel and explored the occult traditions of Greece and the countries around it. In that process, many of the foundations of later occultism took shape.

SEE ALSO: Pythagoras Comes to Crotona (6th Century BCE), Empedocles Invents the Four Elements (5th Century BCE)

A group of philosophers converse at Plato's Academy (Plato is believed to be second from the left) in this first-century Roman mosaic from a villa at Pompeii.

ROME OUTLAWS THE BACCHIC MYSTERIES

RELIGIOUS INTOLERANCE WAS RARE IN ancient times. People who believed in many gods and goddesses rarely took offense if their neighbors prayed to a different set of deities. This tolerance, though, broke down rapidly if a religious movement got involved in politics or crime.

That is what happened to the cult of the Bacchic mysteries in 186 BCE in ancient Rome. It found its way to Italy in the late third century BCE and spread to Rome not long afterward. Originally it admitted only women, held its rituals in the daytime, and did nothing inappropriate. The third priestess of the Bacchic mysteries in Rome, Paculla Annia, began to admit men to the rituals and started holding the ceremonies at night. Later accounts claimed that the rituals turned into orgies and the mystery cult became a criminal organization whose members covered up one another's misdeeds and murdered those who refused to participate.

When rumors reached the Roman authorities, the response was sudden and drastic. The Roman Senate ordered every initiate of the Bacchic mysteries arrested. Some escaped, but more than six thousand were arrested; more than half of them were found guilty of criminal activities and put to death, and the Bacchic mysteries were outlawed throughout Roman territory.

The most important consequence of the prohibition of the Bacchic mysteries, though, was the legal precedent it set. Thereafter, Roman law considered secret religious ceremonies as a potential criminal and political threat, and any religious group that held rituals in private was automatically suspect. That precedent helped drive the persecution of Christians in the early Roman Empire, but it also was applied to the traditions that gave birth to occultism and in that way helped lay the foundations for witch burnings fifteen centuries later.

SEE ALSO: End of the Eleusinian Mysteries (396)

In this fresco from c. 30 BCE—part of the collection of the British Museum—Bacchus, god of wine, pours wine for a panther, while Silenus plays the lyre. Wine played a large role in initiating members into the cult of the Bacchic mysteries.

MIRIAM THE ALCHEMIST

ONE OF THE GREAT CITIES OF THE ANCIENT world, founded by Alexander the Great on the Mediterranean coast of Egypt, Alexandria became the main point of contact between the religious and magical teachings of the Egyptians and the philosophies and initiations of the Greeks. From the bubbling cauldron of traditions that resulted from that blending came many core elements of Western occultism, among them alchemy.

Alchemy was (and is) considerably more than the attempt to turn base metals into gold. To an alchemist, all material things ripen toward perfection unless something gets in the way. The alchemist's mission is to remove the obstacles that keep material things from attaining their perfection. For metals, that perfection is gold; for the human body, health; for the human spirit, union with the divine—and all these and many more are appropriate goals for alchemical work.

To enable material substances to achieve perfection, certain pieces of laboratory gear are needed. Some of the most important of these devices were invented some time in the first century BCE by a Jewish alchemist in Alexandria, a woman named Miriam.

Little is known about the life of Mary the Jewess, as she generally is called in later alchemical writings. The fact that she was a brilliant inventor, though, is clear from the devices she created. One of them, the *kerotakis*, allowed metals to be exposed to corrosive vapors without letting those vapors get into the alchemist's lungs. Another, a still with three spouts at different heights, was the first equipment for fractional distillation. Her most famous creation, though, was the *balneum Mariae*, "Miriam's bath," the double boiler. She invented it to provide steady, even heat to alchemical processes; chefs use it today to cook delicate sauces without burning them—and the French still call this device a *bain-marie*.

SEE ALSO: Zosimos of Panopolis (c. 300)

Illustration of Mary the Jewess from *Symbola aureae mensae duodecim nationum (Symbols of the Golden Table of Twelve Nations)*, 1617, by German alchemist Michael Maier.

DEATH OF JESUS

ACCORDING TO HIS FOUR OFFICIAL BIOG-raphers and the faith of twenty centuries of devout believers, Yeshua bin Maryam, now more commonly known as Jesus Christ, was the son of God, born to a Jewish virgin, who performed miracles, founded the Christian religion, and died on the Cross to redeem humanity. That understanding is so deeply engrained in the cultures of the Western world that it can be a shock to realize that for centuries after his lifetime, a great many people in the Roman world interpreted Jesus in a very different way—as a practitioner of magic.

Jewish literature from the first century CE names him Jesus ben Pantera, the illegitimate son of a Roman soldier by a Jewish woman, who went to Egypt as a migrant worker, learned magic there, and attracted a following after his return to Judea. The identical story appears in the surviving fragments of a work by the pagan philosopher Celsus, *Against the Christians*. Many early Christian writers mentioned versions of this belief, as it was one of the principal arguments against which they had to contend. Other mages apparently shared the same opinion; the name of Jesus appears early and often on amulets and in books of spells as a word of power that can be used to command spirits, and two of the three earliest portrayals of the Crucifixion are on magical amulets, surrounded by incantations.

This narrative—that Jesus of Nazareth was a Jewish sorcerer whose followers redefined him as a god after his death—presented a struggle for newborn Christianity. In fact, this belief probably played an important role in the fear and hatred with which mainstream Christianity has regarded occultism ever since.

SEE ALSO: Apollonius of Tyana (1st Century CE), Basilides of Alexandria (c. 120)

The Crucifixion, c. 1510, a painting by the sixteenth-century Italian artist known as the Master of the Risen Magdalen, from the Yale University Art Gallery.

FALL OF MONA

WHEN GREEKS AND ROMANS FIRST made their way to the Celtic nations of Gaul (today's France), Britain, and Ireland, they found a caste of scholars and loremasters known as Druids. That term probably meant something like "wise ones of the oak," but no one today knows for sure; this is one of the many mysteries surrounding the ancient Druids.

At first, literate people in the Greek and Roman worlds were fascinated by the Druids and assigned them the same status that twentieth-century Americans gave to gurus from India. That changed as Rome targeted the Celtic lands for conquest. In 121 BCE, the Romans seized part of southern Gaul; between 58 and 51 BCE, Julius Caesar conquered the rest of Gaul and carried out two raids on Britain; in 43 CE, the invasion of Britain began in earnest, and by 48 all of what is now England and portions of Scotland and Wales were in Roman hands.

The Druids played an important role in the resistance to Roman invasion in Gaul and Britain, helping to rally the defenders and coordinate military actions between different tribes. In response, Rome targeted the Druids for extermination. Roman edicts proscribed the Druids of Gaul as soon as Julius Caesar's conquest was complete, and in Britain the destruction of the Druids and their sacred places proceeded along with the conquest.

The final blow came in 57 when a Roman force crossed the strait from northern Wales to the island of Mona, a Druid holy place that had become the last refuge of the embattled Druids. The Roman victory there was followed by a general massacre. Thereafter Druids remained only in Ireland, Scotland, and the unconquered hill country of Wales until Christian missionaries penetrated where Roman legions could not go.

SEE ALSO: Druids Celebrate the Autumn Equinox (1798)

Druids, or British Priests, by German-born lithographer Joseph Martin Kronheim (1810–1896), a color plate from his 1868 book *Pictures of English History*.

INVENTION OF THE RUNES

I know that I hung | on the windy tree
  Nine full nights,
Pierced by a spear | offered to Odin
  Myself to myself,
Upon that tree | of which none knows
  Where its roots run. . . .

IN THESE LINES, PART OF THE OLD NORSE POEM *Havamal* (*Words of the High One*), the god Odin described the act of self-sacrifice that won him the runes, the magical alphabet of the Germanic peoples. For more than a thousand years, descendants of those tribes in central Europe, Scandinavia, and Britain used the stark, angular runic letters for religious and magical as well as practical purposes.

Historians, who have to depend on written records and archaeological evidence rather than the words of pagan deities, have traced the origin of the runes to what is now southern Germany some time before 50 CE, the date of the first known runic inscription. Once invented, it quickly took on important symbolic, spiritual, and magical roles and kept those roles through the migrations that followed the collapse of Rome and the long and troubled dark age that ensued.

Runic alphabets were called futharks or futhorcs after the first six runes, which stand for the sounds *f*, *u*, *th*, *a* or *o*, *r*, and *c* or *k*. The oldest known version of the runes, the elder futhark, had twenty-four letters; the younger futhark of Viking times had only sixteen, and the Anglo-Saxon peoples who settled England after the fall of the Roman empire went in the other direction and created the Anglo-Saxon futhorc of twenty-nine or thirty-three letters.

With the coming of Christianity, the runes dropped from use or went underground along with the rest of the Norse and Germanic pagan traditions. There they would remain until the seventeenth century, when their modern revival began.

SEE ALSO: Johannes Bureus Interprets the Runes (1611), Guido von List's Vision of the Runes (1902), Ralph Blum's *The Book of Runes* (1983)

Detail of the Røk Runestone at Røk, Östergötland, Sweden. Thought to date from the early 800s, this famous runestone features the longest-known runic inscription in stone and is considered to mark the beginning of Swedish literature.

APOLLONIUS OF TYANA

VERY LITTLE IS KNOWN FOR CERTAIN about the most famous mage of the Roman world. The biography of Apollonius of Tyana (c. 15 CE–c. 100 CE) was written more than a century after his death by the Greek author Philostratus, who—like the biographers of that other miracle worker from the first century CE, Jesus of Nazareth— packed the tale with exciting stories but never got around to including many historical details.

He was born in the town of Tyana in what is now southern Turkey. In his adolescent years, he was deeply impressed by the teachings of Pythagoras and decided to become a disciple of the Pythagorean Brotherhood. The fact that the brotherhood no longer existed was no obstacle; Apollonius devoted himself to all the disciplines and austerities Pythagoras would have imposed on him, including the five-year vow of silence.

Later he embarked on travels throughout the Roman world, seeking wisdom, and if Philostratus is to be believed, he even ventured east through the Persian Empire to the distant land of India to study with its sages. All the while, his reputation as a holy man grew. Like Jesus of Nazareth, he was particularly well known for healing the sick and banishing demons, and he was said to have raised a girl from the dead. When a jealous rival got him in trouble with the Roman government, he went to Rome, defended himself before the imperial courts, won an acquittal, and then suddenly disappeared from the courtroom and was seen the same day in another town many miles away. Unlike his partial equivalent from Judea, Apollonius died of old age. For centuries after his time, talismans based on his designs were used to ward off shipwreck, vermin, and dangerous beasts, but no religion was founded in his name.

SEE ALSO: Death of Jesus (33 CE)

Statue of a wandering philosopher, commonly associated with Apollonius of Tyana, at the Heraklion Archaeological Museum in Greece, dating from the late second to third century CE.

Cito Imperatore andando all' impresa di Verusalemme consultò Basilide figlio de Prosti, e Priore del Monte Carmelo per sapere l'euento della Guerra, quale le predisse la vittoria contro li hebrei, esprimendosi che Iddio sdegnato contro di quelli, per la morte che haueuano
a Christo si douena sedesser la giustitia diuina con fulminar dardi contro Verusalemme.   Disegno di Pietro Testa, la cui pittura originale si conserua in S. Martino di Monti in Roma.   Franc. Petrarcha de Vespasiano ac Iudea, et Iuda.

Pietro Testa delineauit   R.mo P.re Nic de Carmelitani Gio. Ab.e Felippini Romano   D.D.D. Franc.o Collignon   Gio. Cesaro Roma

BASILIDES OF ALEXANDRIA

PLATO, IN HIS DIALOGUE *THE STATESMAN*, used the term *gnostikoi*—"those capable of knowing"—for the people he thought should run society. Many other philosophers, including Plato's followers, used the same term on and off in the years that followed. Around the beginning of the Christian era, though, it came to have a different meaning: those who were capable of knowing the mysteries of the spiritual world, members of a secretive movement that fused Plato's philosophy with elements from Egyptian, Greek, and Christian thought to create a new spirituality deeply tinged with occultism. We know them today as the Gnostics.

No one is sure where the first Gnostics emerged, but Alexandria is a likely guess. Certainly that was where the first important Gnostic teacher lived and taught. His name was Basilides of Alexandria. The only surviving scraps of his teachings appear in the writings of later Christian heresy hunters, and those records are so sparse that only the bare outlines are clear.

Like later Gnostics, though, Basilides taught that the human soul had descended from a world of light into the darkness of matter and was trapped there by the machinations of an evil god, Yaldabaoth the Demiurge, who had created the material world. Jesus, he taught, had come down from the world of light to teach the fallen how to return to their home. Following the teachings of Jesus as they understood them, Gnostics practiced demanding spiritual disciplines and learned the words of power that would enable them to vanquish Yaldabaoth's demons.

When Gnosticism first emerged, in the second century CE, Christianity was still a scattered sect with no political power and little doctrinal consistency. Most of three centuries would pass before that changed—and when it did, the Gnostics faced savage persecution from orthodox Christians.

SEE ALSO: Valentinus Loses a Papal Election (155), The *Corpus Hermeticum* (3rd Century), The Albigensian Crusade (1208)

c. 120

The Prophecy of Basilides (1630–1660), by Giovanni Cesare Testa, after Pietro Testa. In the drawing, Emperor Titus, on his way to Jerusalem, consults Basilides, who shows him a vision of God the Father with the dead Christ.

Apuleius

Lucian

Credo Pudiciam Saturno
Rege Moratam In Terris.
Iuvenal

MAGIC ON TRIAL

IT WAS A MATCH MADE IN HEAVEN, OR SO Lucius Apuleius (c. 124–c. 170) must have thought. On his way home from Athens with his school friend Socinius, he'd fallen sick on the road, and Socinius took him home, where his recently widowed mother, Aemilia, took care of the handsome young student. Aemilia was young, beautiful, well educated, and rich; she and Lucius promptly fell in love and got married.

The fly in the ointment was Aemilia's relatives, who were not amused by the young widow's sudden remarriage. They accused Lucius of using love magic to seduce Aemilia and filed charges with the local Roman officials. The accusation wasn't completely absurd, because Lucius had been studying Platonic philosophy in Athens, and the blending of magic with Plato's philosophy was already well under way by his time.

Fortunately, Lucius also had studied rhetoric and was more than qualified to defend himself in court. When he was brought to trial before the Roman procurator, all charges were dismissed. Lucius's speech survives and provides an intriguing glimpse into beliefs about occultism in the heyday of Rome.

Lucius and Aemilia then did the sensible thing and moved away from her relatives. They settled at Carthage, where he became a famous orator, teacher, and author. His most famous book, the only surviving Roman novel, is *The Golden Ass*; it tells the story of a young idiot named Lucius who is turned into a donkey by a witch and goes through a series of madcap adventures before being returned to human form by the goddess Isis. Like Lucius's speech, it contains a great deal of information about occultism in Roman times.

SEE ALSO: Death of Plato (347 BCE), Plotinus Begins Teaching in Rome (244)

The frontispiece of an 1821 edition of *The Golden Ass*, also known as the *Metamorphoses* of Apuleius, the only surviving Roman novel in Latin.

Pius

VALENTINUS LOSES A PAPAL ELECTION

ORN IN A SMALL TOWN IN EGYPT'S NILE delta, Valentinus (c. 100–c. 160) went to Alexandria to seek an education. A devout Christian and before long an ordained priest, he studied with Theudas, one of the original disciples of the Apostle Paul, and gained a reputation for scholarship and personal sanctity—but like many Christians at that time, he was also a Gnostic.

In 136, he went to Rome. Those were the years when authority among Christians in the western half of the empire was starting to centralize, and the position of bishop of Rome had begun to turn into the office of pope. Valentinus hoped to inherit that office on the death of the incumbent, Hyginus.

When Hyginus died in 142, however, Pius I was elected in his place. Pius was a fierce opponent of Gnosticism and one of the leading champions of what would become Christian orthodoxy in the years to come; his election was a blow to the entire Gnostic movement. Valentinus was still relatively young, though, and he remained in Rome, teaching and writing, in the hope that the death of Pius would clear the way to the papacy.

When Pius I died in 155, however, Anicetus—another orthodox churchman—was elected in his place. Valentinus left Rome shortly afterward and went to the island of Cyprus, where he taught until his death. In the wake of his defeat, his many followers left Christian congregations to found churches of their own. Believers in other, alternative versions of Christian teachings did the same thing, and in their absence, the drift of the Christian church toward a harshly defended dogmatism proceeded unchecked.

SEE ALSO: Basilides of Alexandria (c. 120)

Pope Pius I, from the workshop of Michel Wolgemut, used as an illustration in the book *Liber chronicarum* (or the *Nuremberg Chronicle*) by Hartmann Schedel, published in Latin and German in 1493.

HERMES MERCURIUS TRIMEGISTUS
CONTEMPORANEUS MOYSI

DEUS OMNIUM CREATOR
SECUM DEUM FECIT
VISIBILEM ET HUNC
FECIT PRIMUM ET SOLUM
QUO OBLECTATUS EST ET
VALDE AMAVIT PROPRIUM
FILIUM QUI APPELLATUR
SANCTUM VERBUM

CASTISSIMVM VIR
GINIS TEMPLVM
CASTE MEMENTO
INGREDI

THE CORPUS HERMETICUM

THE FUSION OF GREEK PHILOSOPHY AND Egyptian mystery teachings that gave rise to alchemy and Gnosticism had other consequences, one of which would have an immense influence on the history of occultism. This was a collection of writings called the *Corpus Hermeticum*, a set of fifteen short treatises supposedly written by an Egyptian sage named Hermes Trismegistus in ancient times. They were actually the product of a school of mystics that flourished in Egypt between the first and third centuries of the common era who credited the legendary founder of their school with the authorship of all their writings.

Like the Gnostics, the followers of Hermes believed that humanity descended into the world of matter from a higher realm and could find salvation only by rising above matter. They rejected the Gnostic claim that the universe was the evil creation of an evil god, though, and taught self-discipline, occult philosophy, alchemy, astrology, and magic, which would lead to a rebirth in which the initiate reconnected with the spiritual realm and its divine powers.

Copies of the *Corpus Hermeticum*, along with many other writings of the same general sort, spread widely through the Roman world during the last centuries of paganism and played a significant role in the occult spirituality of that era. The most important impact of the *Corpus Hermeticum* on the history of occultism, though, came many centuries later. One copy of the collection survived the centuries of Christian persecution of occultism and eventually found its way to Renaissance Italy. When it was translated, the vision of a spirituality centered on occultism burst like a bombshell over the European world and set traditions in motion that are still alive.

SEE ALSO: Zosimos of Panopolis (c. 300), Translation of the *Corpus Hermeticum* (1464), Casting Spells for the Pope (1628)

Hermes Trismegistus, supposed author of the *Corpus Hermeticum*, as seen in this 1488 marble detail by Giovanni di Stefano da Siena (c. 1446–c. 1506).

PLOTINUS BEGINS TEACHING IN ROME

BY THE THIRD CENTURY CE, THE GREAT age of classical philosophy was long past, but many people in the Roman Empire still read the Greek philosophers and discussed their teachings. A capable thinker with a unique take on the core questions of philosophy could attract an audience and found a school, and that was what Plotinus did when he arrived in Rome in 244 CE.

Plotinus (c. 205–270) was born in Egypt and studied in Alexandria for eleven years with Ammonius, an important Platonist philosopher. In 243, he joined Emperor Gordian's invasion of the Persian Empire, but Gordian was assassinated by his own soldiers and Plotinus had a difficult time making his way back to safety within Roman borders. This experience seems to have cured him of any further taste for adventure; he settled in Rome and began offering lectures on philosophy shortly afterward and stayed there until just before his death.

His teachings started from Plato's basic division between the world of Being and the world of Becoming but unfolded them in a more mystical direction. He taught his students to use contemplation to commune with the world of Being, and he also portrayed the basic patterns of the world of Being as intelligent beings; later generations would identify them as the gods and goddesses of pagan religion or the angels and archangels of the Christian faith. He criticized the Gnostics harshly, but his own teaching had important features in common with theirs, including a great interest in how magic and astrology worked.

Plotinus's revision of Plato's teaching, which is called Neoplatonism by modern scholars, became the last great school of philosophy in the classical world. It also became the foundation on which most later occultists based their theories and practices.

SEE ALSO: Death of Plato (347 BCE), Basilides of Alexandria (c. 120), Death of Iamblichus of Chalcis (330)

A Roman marble bust of a philosopher believed to be Plotinus, created c. 350.

Τοῦ ἄνω ὑπεράδεξεως ὁτα εχοντας ηχετθητσ το
χαλκα ουετ ωνιαλῶ ωπαδος ο στραμικης εχουσ
Ποθραμισουπτηριαπλῶσατας οσιμβολαοαεγθε
επτα ακρατω γου ωληγ υβηλουὑαπολολο
μιαχω ποαχῆς ϊναμηραγλῶοϊναπογτη
θερμης του ϋδατος κομηζουσης το αυαβαινου· το
δε σχῆμα τουτο λιχαγος ουληκ· Επιδεηχ
λος ρο ποσκομηδη εν υδατος θθεμ εχλου χωρι
βηκος· επτοσωληγ ἐς τωθμηελα χαλκιουευπεθτ
μι βηκος πηλεος α ς· τωλπι ρο πτχη
χος ςζ κ υποκατω χω ωπτα αθ ουαπτιρου· φεμη
οπιαρμοξ ς το χελχχα ογχηθ δε ηχαλχοι ςτετπτη
κηρω η τπηλῶ, η ως βουλη κκ καμ ονο αμα σασ
οιδε τυπιοι ουτοι·—

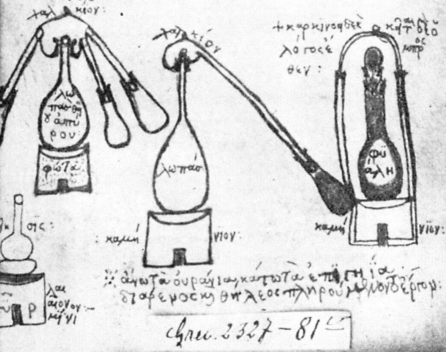

: ἀγει τα ουρἀνια και κἀτω τα ἐπι γη ϊα
ρ αφερος κη θηλεος πληρουλων λουθεργον·

ZOSIMOS OF PANOPOLIS

Four centuries after the time of Miriam the Alchemist, alchemy was still thriving in the great Egyptian metropolis of Alexandria, and it was there that one of the most important ancient alchemical authors thrived around the year 300 CE. His name was Zosimos, he was born in the town of Panopolis in the southern part of Egypt, and he visited the ancient city of Memphis to inspect an ancient alchemical furnace; those are essentially the only facts about his life that survive.

His writings, however, reveal much about the Alexandrian alchemical scene in his time. He had access to the writings of many previous alchemists and considered the work of Miriam the Alchemist particularly valuable. He also knew the spiritual literature of his time and was strongly influenced by the *Corpus Hermeticum*, which he quoted with approval in several places. To him, alchemy dealt as much with spiritual transformation as with material substances. Some of his most influential writings took the form of vivid dream sequences in which mysterious persons and places hinted at the deeper secrets of alchemy. Whether or not he was the first to do this, his writings played an important role in making myth, metaphor, and symbolic imagery central to later alchemical literature.

Several of Zosimos's books were addressed to another alchemist: a woman named Theosebia who was a respected teacher of alchemy. The two of them apparently had a running disagreement about secrecy; Theosebia held the traditional view that alchemy was only to be passed on to select pupils under an oath of silence, whereas Zosimos believed that alchemy ought to be shared with all. No record survives of Theosebia's side of the argument, but history shows that her point of view won the debate.

SEE ALSO: Miriam the Alchemist (1st Century BCE), The *Corpus Hermeticum* (3rd Century)

A fifteenth-century Byzantine Greek manuscript page illustrating Zosimos's distillation equipment.

C. 300

PORPHIRE SOPHISTE.
Chap. 37.

POVR ce que traictant cy deuāt les mœurs & vertuz de ce grand docteur Origene, i'ay cité comme tesmoignage valable, l'opinion qu'auoit de luy Porphire Philosophe Tyrien, ioinct que parmy mes autres recherches est tombé entre mes mains son pourtraict naturel, que i'ay recouuert d'vn Grec estant en la ville de Retimo, située en l'Isle de Crete, il ne m'a semblé impertinent vous le representer, & traicter superficielement de luy, non pour le loüer, ains affin de mōstrer que

DEATH OF IAMBLICHUS OF CHALCIS

BY THE LATE THIRD CENTURY, Christianity was a rising power throughout the Roman world. Unlike pagan religions, Christianity wasn't committed to a crumbling status quo. Its appeal to the poor and downtrodden made it immensely attractive in an age of social and economic turmoil, but there were still plenty of people whose loyalty lay with the old ways and who sought to unite pagans in a defensive alliance against the new faith.

The most successful of them was Iamblichus of Chalcis (c. 250–330). Born into an upper-class family in Roman Syria, he studied Plato's philosophy with the great teachers Anatolius and Porphyry. In his youth, philosophy and pagan religion were still at odds with each other; his teacher Porphyry, for example, denounced the traditional pagan custom of animal sacrifice. Iamblichus, by contrast, set out to find common ground between philosophy and religion.

He did that by completing the fusion of Platonic philosophy and occultism. Iamblichus saw that the traditional magical and religious practices of the ancient world could be reimagined as aids to the mystical vision of reality Plato and Plotinus had discussed. He named this new application of magic *theurgy*, "the divine work." In his writings, especially *On the Mysteries*, he explained how every aspect of traditional pagan religion and magic made sense in Platonic terms and therefore could be practiced and defended by intellectuals as well as ordinary Romans.

Iamblichus was swimming against the tide, and his attempt to counter the spread of Christianity with a resurgent paganism would fail. In the short term, though, it sparked the last great upsurge in classical occultism—and in the long term, his writings and the theurgy he taught would become powerful influences on occult traditions millennia later.

SEE ALSO: Death of Plato (347 BCE), Plotinus Begins Teaching in Rome (244), Thomas Taylor Translates *On the Mysteries* (1821)

An illustration of Porphyry from *Les vrais pourtraits et vies des hommes illustres Grecz, Latins et payens* (*The True Portraits and Lives of Illustrious Greek, Latin, and Pagan Men*), published in 1584 by French Franciscan explorer and cosmographer André Thévet. Iamblichus was Porphyry's student, although he later developed his own belief system.

LAST PAGAN EMPEROR OF ROME

I N 313, THE ROMAN EMPEROR CONSTANTINE issued the Edict of Milan, removing all legal penalties against Christianity and giving the Christian church a variety of privileges. Christians responded by going on the offensive against paganism, supported by the imperial government, which made Christian monks and priests immune from prosecution. Before the triumph of the new religion, however, an improbable series of events brought a pagan philosopher to the throne.

As a son of Constantine's half brother, Julian (c. 331–363) received a pious Christian education but rejected Christianity in favor of the old pagan gods. He studied in Ephesus and Athens and embraced the magical Neoplatonism that Iamblichus had taught.

Then a new emperor, Constantine's son Constantius II, placed Julian in charge of Britain and Gaul. The young man turned out to be a competent general and administrator, defeating barbarians on the frontier and reforming the local government. Constantius,

a fanatical Christian, became jealous of his cousin; Julian's soldiers proclaimed him emperor, and when Constantius died suddenly in 361, the whole Roman world acknowledged Julian as the heir of the Caesars.

He moved quickly to proclaim toleration for all religions, reinstate pagan temples and priesthoods where they had been abolished, and remove privilege from the Christian clergy. In 362, though, rising tensions with the Persian Empire forced him to leave the capital at Constantinople and join the armies in the east. Early the next year he led the Roman armies to victory near Ctesiphon but was mortally wounded shortly afterward. With him died the last hope of classical paganism, and his involvement with theurgy helped lay the groundwork for the centuries of persecution that occultism suffered thereafter.

SEE ALSO: Plotinus Begins Teaching in Rome (244), Death of Iamblichus of Chalcis (330)

A bust of fourth-century Roman Emperor Julian the Apostate, from the Musei Capitolini, Rome, Italy.

END OF THE ELEUSINIAN MYSTERIES

FOR TWO THOUSAND YEARS, MAYBE MORE, the ceremonies had been celebrated every autumn in the small town of Eleusis near Athens, becoming more famous and elaborate with the passing years. By Roman times, the mystery temple at Eleusis was a huge building half the size of a football field, and people came there from the far corners of the ancient world.

All new initiates had to go through preliminary ceremonies at the river Ilissos in the month of Anthesterion, our February, in which they offered sacrifices, cleansed themselves in the water, and listened to instruction. A year and a half later, in Boedromion (our September), they marched to Eleusis, arriving at dusk. They entered the temple, and the ceremony of initiation was enacted. No one today knows what it was, but ancient writers agreed that those who passed through it had no fear of death afterward.

Even after Christianity seized power, the mysteries of Eleusis continued for a time and then flourished anew during Julian's brief reign. When a new emperor issued an edict in 384 prohibiting nocturnal pagan meetings, the proconsul of Greece, Vettius Agorius Praetextatus, defied the order at the risk of his life and position. Still, politics among the remaining pagans and increasing pressure from Christian zealots troubled the last years of the mysteries.

Finally, in 396, the barbarian Visigoths invaded Greece. They were recent converts to Christianity and looted and wrecked pagan sanctuaries throughout the country, including Eleusis. Though small groups of pagans kept up a semblance of the old rites elsewhere for many years thereafter, the destruction of the temple marked the end of the Eleusinian mysteries in their traditional form.

SEE ALSO: Rome Outlaws the Bacchic Mysteries (186 BCE)

Fourth-century votive plaque, known as the Ninnion Tablet, depicting initiation rites of the Eleusinian Mysteries, kept at the National Archaeological Museum in Athens.

THE EDICTS OF JUSTINIAN

NONE OF THE REMAINING PAGANS IN THE Roman world had any doubt about what was coming, but the end still must have been a shock. In 538, the Emperor Justinian stripped every non-Christian and every Christian heretic in the empire of all their civil rights and ordered the closing of every pagan educational and cultural institution. Protests on the part of the pagan minority were suppressed by government troops, and the long history of paganism in the ancient world was over.

In response, some of the remaining pagans chose a desperate expedient and journeyed eastward to the borders of the empire. Some found a home in the Persian Empire, which had a far more tolerant attitude toward religion than Rome did. Others traveled farther still, into central Asia and the outermost provinces of the Chinese Empire, where Christian heresies also found a welcoming home. A significant number, though, settled in Harran.

This town had existed since the third millennium BCE, nestled in a valley in what is now southeastern Turkey: a city of mud brick houses surrounded by green fields and low brown hills. The Sumerians who founded it as a trading post dedicated it to their moon god, Sin, but it absorbed religious and magical traditions from countless peoples as the Middle East passed through the long cycles of its history.

The coming of Christianity and the legal proscription of paganism had surprisingly little impact on Harran. A border town on the troubled frontier between the Roman and Persian empires, it could afford to ignore Roman laws banning pagan worship. Over the years that followed, Harran became the last holdout of the pagan Neoplatonism of Iamblichus and Julian, teaching a version of pagan worship laced with occult teachings and practices.

SEE ALSO: Fall of Harran (1271)

A mosaic panel, executed in 547, depicting Emperor Justinian I, at the Basilica of San Vitale in Ravenna, Italy.

Merlinus

MERLIN AND THE BATTLE OF ARDERYDD

IS REAL NAME WAS PROBABLY A ROUNDED-off form of Ambrosius and he never met the hard-bitten Roman-British warlord who is remembered now as King Arthur, but Merlin the enchanter was apparently a real person. He lived in the Scottish Lowlands during the sixth century, and fragments of his biography survived long enough to be woven into a romance by the medieval author Geoffrey of Monmouth.

Britain in the sixth century was ravaged by warfare. Saxon warriors from what is now the northwestern coast of Germany had been invited there to serve as a mercenary force, only to turn on their employers and carve out territories for themselves. The British people were unable to unite against the Saxons for many reasons, including religious strife that divided Christians from pagans and set them at war with one another. In 573, at the battle of Arderydd, the last pagan ruler in Britain south of the Highlands was defeated and killed by a Christian army. The king's name was Gwenddolau, and the original Merlin was his court poet and, very possibly, his Druid priest; Merlin's elegy for the fallen king is among the oldest surviving poems in the Welsh language.

How Merlin's story got attached to the body of tales surrounding King Arthur is hard to say, but such things have happened many times in the history of legends. Once he got attached to the enormously popular Arthurian stories, though, Merlin quickly became the archetype on which most later wizards were modeled, and prophecies ghostwritten for him by industrious authors became as popular in the Middle Ages as the predictions of Nostradamus are today.

SEE ALSO: Fall of Mona (57 CE)

An illustration of Merlin from the *Nuremberg Chronicle*, a world history and biblical paraphrase written by Hartmann Schedel, 1493.

GEBER ALCHYMISTE ARABE.
Chap. 33.

JABIR IBN HAYYAN

H E WAS ONE OF THE GREATEST SCHOLARS of his age, the author of more than a hundred books on a galaxy of subjects, but Jabir ibn Hayyan's great passion was alchemy. Born in Kufa in what is now Iraq, Jabir ibn Hayyan (c. 720–c. 815) took up the study of medicine and for many years was a respected physician in his hometown. Later in life—the exact date is not known—he was invited to Baghdad, the political capital of the Muslim world, by the caliph Harun al-Rashid.

By the time Jabir arrived in Baghdad, the great age of Muslim conquests was over. Although the pagan religions of Greece and Rome were strictly forbidden, the philosophical and scientific knowledge amassed by Greek and Roman scholars was not, and many branches of occultism were taken up by Arab scholars along with other relics of classical learning. Alchemy and astrology in particular attracted the attention of Muslim intellectuals; once the surviving knowledge base had been mastered, a great deal of original work was done on both of those branches of occult study.

Jabir's arrival in Baghdad was part of that process. With the caliph's financial backing, he set up the most complete alchemical laboratory of that time and carried out an ambitious program of experiments. His goal was not merely to make gold but to understand the inner nature of metals and the natural world as a whole. He developed new methods for preparing a range of useful chemicals, devised ingenious furnaces to produce steady heat for alchemical processes, and proposed theories about the composition of metals that remained in place until the coming of the scientific revolution.

SEE ALSO: Miriam the Alchemist (1st Century BCE), Zosimos of Panopolis (c. 300)

c. 800 CE

Jabir ibn Hayyan, also known by the Latin name Geber, seen here with his alchemical equipment in an engraving from 1584 by French historian André Thévet.

CANON *EPISCOPI*

Certain wicked women . . . believe and profess that in the hours of the night they ride out on certain animals with Diana, the goddess of the Pagans, and an innumerable multitude of other women, and in the silence of the dead of night they journey over vast distances of the earth, and obey her commands as their mistress, and are summoned to her service on certain nights.

THESE WORDS COME FROM A DECISION made by a local church council in France during the ninth century. Later the decision was mistakenly attributed to the Council of Ancyra in the fourth century, one of the ecumenical councils that established the foundations of Christianity. In this form it became part of Catholic canon law. The text begins with the word *bishops—episcopi* in Latin—and that gave the decision its enduring name: the canon *Episcopi*.

The beliefs of the "wicked women" were not unique to ninth-century France. Across Europe, legends and church records tell of a body of shamanistic beliefs in which certain people left their bodies at night on certain dates to travel in the company of supernatural beings. To this day, no one knows for sure what lies behind those traditions.

What gives the canon *Episcopi* its importance in the history of occultism, though, is that it dismissed the beliefs of the "wicked women" as superstition or, at most, hallucinations inspired by the Devil and declared it sinful to believe that witches had any power to harm Christians. Through most of the Middle Ages, as a result, Catholic religious authorities dismissed witchcraft beliefs and other occult traditions as foolish notions held only by the ignorant. It was not until the fourteenth century that the canon *Episcopi* was set aside and the Burning Times began.

SEE ALSO: Cecco d'Ascoli Burned at the Stake (1327), The *Benandanti* (1575)

Diana as Personification of the Night, c. 1765, one of an ensemble of four paintings by Anton Raphael Mengs (1728–1779). In the ninth century, some "wicked women" claimed to take to the skies to do Diana's bidding.

FOUNDING OF THE KNIGHTS TEMPLAR

THERE WERE ONLY NINE OF THEM AT first—knights from France who joined the First Crusade to seize the Holy Land from the Muslims. In 1118 they went before the Patriarch of Jerusalem and formed an order of warrior monks, combining the discipline of the cloister with that of the battlefield. They were assigned quarters on the site of the ruined Temple of Solomon and took the name the Order of the Poor Knights of Christ and the Temple of Solomon. History remembers them as the Knights Templar.

Their official mission was to protect pilgrims against Muslim raiders on the dangerous trip from the ports on the Mediterranean coast. Nine knights constituted too small a force to guard the pilgrim routes, though, and for the first nine years the Templars seem to have made no effort to increase their number. Long-standing rumors—backed up by archaeological evidence—suggest that much of their time was spent tunneling beneath the temple ruins.

What they found there remains a mystery. In 1127, though, the Grand Master of the little order, Hugues de Payens (c. 1070–1136), returned to France. Thereafter new recruits flocked to the Templar banner, and kings and nobles bestowed lavish gifts on the order. The Poor Knights quickly became one of the richest monastic orders in Christendom. Templar properties across Europe funneled income to the Templar castles that guarded the Holy Land; the flow of funds was so great that the Knights Templar invented most of the principles of modern banking to handle them. Every time you sign a check, you're making use of a Templar technique.

In all this there was no hint of occultism. That would come later, after generations of Templars had lived in the religious and magical melting pot of the Holy Land, and would set in motion a legend and a legacy that endure to this day.

SEE ALSO: Arrest of the Knights Templar (1307)

1118

The Knights Templar were a wealthy and powerful order known for their battles in the Crusades and management of economic infrastructure, until they were eventually arrested and burned at the stake.

THE ALBIGENSIAN CRUSADE

THEY CALLED THEMSELVES CATHARS, from the Greek word for "pure ones"; their enemies called them Albigensians, "those people from Albi," after the French town where their early activities were centered. They taught a Gnostic Christianity in which God and Satan were equally matched, and human beings, imprisoned in Satan's world of matter, were called to escape to God's world of light. They rejected the authority of the pope and the sacraments of the Catholic Church. Despite this, they established a foothold in northern Italy and southern France beginning around the year 1000. From 1175 on, corruption among the Catholic clergy and effective preaching on the part of the Cathars led to dramatic growth of the movement. Rome responded by condemning Catharism as heresy and sending missionaries to counter it, but those actions did little to slow the spread of the movement.

In 1208, the rising spiral of tension broke into open violence when a papal legate was murdered by Cathars. In response, Pope Innocent III proclaimed a crusade. All previous crusades had been directed against the Muslims in the Holy Land; this was the first time the church had called for war against its enemies in Europe—but not the last. Fighting began in 1209 and raged until the last Cathar stronghold, Montségur, fell in 1244. In the course of the war, the south of France was devastated and hundreds of thousands of innocent civilians died.

Among the legacies of the Albigensian crusade was a new organization, which was founded by the Catholic Church in 1239 and tasked with hunting down heretics by any means necessary. Over the following centuries, that organization would leave a trail of blood across Europe, and thousands of occultists, among many others, would be condemned by it to a fiery death. Its name, of course, was the Inquisition.

SEE ALSO: Basilides of Alexandria (c. 120)

St. Dominic de Guzman and the Albigensians, painted by Pedro Berruguete in the late fifteenth century. The painting depicts a legend in which, during a dispute between St. Dominic and the Cathars, the books of both were thrown onto the flames—and those of the saint were miraculously spared.

PORTAE LVCIS

Hęc est porta Tetragrámaton iusti intrabūt per eam.

זה השער לי-הוה צדיקים יבאו בו

ORIGINS OF THE CABALA

EVERYBODY IN THE JEWISH COMMUNITY of Narbonne in the south of France knew that Rabbi Isaac the Blind (c. 1160–c. 1235) was a profound scholar who knew an enormous amount about the scriptures. Only among his inner circle of students, though, had rumors begun to spread that the respected rabbi was on to something far deeper and more exciting than the normal process of scriptural interpretation: a new way of understanding the Torah that seemed to open the door to astonishing mysteries.

As the early history of the Cathar heresy showed, the southern provinces of France had a tolerant attitude toward dissidence. Jewish communities thrived there, and trade links with North Africa and the Levant brought knowledge that was lost in Europe's Dark Ages but had survived in the Muslim world. It was in that way that rabbis in southern France obtained two ancient books—the *Sepher yetzirah* (*Book of Formation*) and the *Sepher ha-bahir* (*Book of Splendor*)—that hinted at profound secrets hidden in the scriptures.

The secret to Rabbi Isaac's new teaching, though, was numerical: the same traditions of number mysticism and sacred geometry that had entered the Western world with Pythagoras and played an important role in Gnosticism. He and his students came to believe that these were the keys to the innermost teachings of Judaism and were so precious that they could be handed down only by word of mouth. Before long, the Hebrew word for "oral tradition"—which can be spelled Cabala, Kabbalah, or Qabalah in English—came to be applied to those teachings. After Rabbi Isaac's death, they spread rapidly through Jewish communities around the Mediterranean. Centuries would pass, though, before the Cabala became a core element of the wider occult traditions of the Western world.

SEE ALSO: Abraham Abulafia Goes to Saronno (1279), Johannes Reuchlin's *On the Miraculous Word* (1494), Isaac Luria Arrives in Safed (1570)

This diagram of the Sefirothic Tree, from Paulus Ricius's *Portae Lucis* (1516), depicts the divine attributes, the Jewish mystical system of the Cabala.

TRANSLATION OF *PICATRIX*

SPAIN IN THE THIRTEENTH CENTURY WAS A patchwork of warring kingdoms, but one of them—Castile—saw a remarkable flowering of art, scholarship, and occultism. Under the patronage of King Alfonso X (1221–1284), called *el Sabio* (the Wise), many works on occultism were translated from Arabic. The most important was a strange book with an indecipherable title: *Picatrix*.

The Arabic original was titled *Ghayat al-hakim* (*The Goal of the Sage*). It was written in the ninth or tenth century by an anonymous Arab wizard in Spain or North Africa who hid his identity behind the name of the distinguished scholar and mystic al-Majriti. Nobody knows why Alfonso's translators changed the title or what the word *Picatrix* means. What made *Picatrix* so important was that it was an encyclopedic manual of magical philosophy and practice, the most comprehensive work on occultism to appear in the Western world between Iamblichus's *On the Mysteries* and Cornelius Agrippa's *Three Books of Occult Philosophy*.

The teachings of *Picatrix* focused on astrology, but an astrology worlds away from the modern practice of reading personality from a birth chart. Instead, the heavens were sources of magical power, and ceremonies performed when the planets were in certain positions drew down the power of the stars to make marvels happen on earth. To turn the pages of *Picatrix* today is to be transported into a world of talismans, potions, and perilous spirits that can help magicians or, if a single detail of the ritual is omitted, destroy them.

Once it was translated into Latin, *Picatrix* became the most notorious sorcerer's manual in the Western world. Few dared to admit that they owned a copy, but most of the important magical handbooks of the time borrowed freely from it. Not until the widespread abandonment of occultism at the end of the Renaissance did it fall into obscurity.

SEE ALSO: Cornelius Agrippa's *Three Books of Occult Philosophy* (1533), Thomas Taylor Translates *On the Mysteries* (1821)

Portrait of King Alfonso X, also known as el Sabio, by Spanish painter Joaquín Domínguez Bécquer (1817–1879). During his rein in Castile, many important occult works were translated from Arabic.

FALL OF HARRAN

THE TOWN OF HARRAN HAD ENDURED FOR millennia despite the rise and fall of empires and civilizations. Its position on the borderland between the Roman and Persian empires made it a refuge for pagans after the Roman Empire proscribed every religion but Christianity, and for many centuries it remained a haven not only for pagan religion but also for the theurgic occult traditions Iamblichus had woven into the older pagan faiths.

When the armies of Islam conquered the region in 639 CE, once again Harran endured. The Quran requires Muslims to tolerate three "religions of the book": Judaism, Christianity, and *Sabi'ah* or Sabianism. What exactly *Sabi'ah* is or was has perplexed Muslim scholars for many centuries, but the people of Harran managed to convince their Arab conquerors that Allah had them in mind and were allowed to keep their religious traditions unhindered.

For more than six centuries thereafter, Harran thrived as a center of magical, astrological, alchemical, and philosophical studies, and many of its scholars rose to respected positions in the Islamic world. One of them, the famous astrologer Thabit ibn Qurrah (826–901), published a defense of the Harranian religion that was long famous.

Wars between the caliphate of Baghdad and the Byzantine Empire devastated the region, though, and were followed by wars between contending Muslim rulers and finally by the Mongol invasion. The temple of the moon god, the spiritual heart of Harran, was wrecked in the wars, and the trade routes on which Harran's prosperity depended did not survive the turmoil.

In 1271, the city was abandoned by its last residents. Long before that happened, though, the occult traditions that had found a haven there had spread throughout the Muslim world and in due time reached Christian Europe as well.

SEE ALSO: The Edicts of Justinian (538)

The tower and arch of the Temple of Sin, the God of the Moon, at the archaeological site of Harran. The temple was destroyed in wars between contending leaders and with foreign invaders.

הכון לקראת אלהיך ישראל

ABRAHAM ABULAFIA GOES TO SARONNO

FROM ITS ORIGINS IN SOUTHERN FRANCE, the Cabala spread rapidly throughout the Jewish diaspora. Abraham Abulafia (c. 1240–c. 1291) was among its early masters. A rabbi's son from Saragossa in Spain, he studied the Torah and the Talmud with his father until the latter's death in 1258. Thereafter, in the usual fashion of the time, he traveled from place to place, looking for a teacher who could expound the deeper mysteries of the scriptures.

He found what he was looking for in Barcelona in 1271 when a Cabalist named Baruch Togarmi introduced him to the *Sepher yetzirah* and taught him to meditate on combinations of Hebrew letters. Within a short time Abulafia underwent a profound spiritual awakening and came to believe that God had granted him prophetic powers.

In 1279, a visionary experience convinced Abulafia that God had called him to convert Pope Nicholas III to Judaism. He went at once to Rome, where he found that the pope had gone to the town of Saronno, and set out after him. Rumors of his mission reached Saronno before he did, and the pope ordered that Abulafia be seized and burned at the stake if he presented himself at the papal court. Though he was told of this, Abulafia presented himself anyway—and found on his arrival at the court that the pope had died during the night. Church officials imprisoned Abulafia for a month and then let him go.

He returned to Barcelona, but his idiosyncratic beliefs and claims of prophetic powers were too much for the local Jewish community; eventually he relocated to Sicily and then to a little island near Malta. Though he remained a controversial figure, he had no shortage of students, and his meditations on the Hebrew alphabet became a common practice in later Cabalistic schools.

SEE ALSO: Origins of the Cabala (1230), Johannes Reuchlin's *On the Miraculous Word* (1494), Isaac Luria Arrives in Safed (1570)

An illuminated page from *Light of the Intellect* by Abraham Abulafia (1285).

Ne cest an aussi ou mops de mars
ou temps de karesme. le general
maistre du temple et vn autre
grant maistre apres lui en lordze si cõme len dit
uisiteur a vaus en lisse devant les augustins

ARREST OF THE KNIGHTS TEMPLAR

T HE ORDERS WENT OUT SECRETLY FROM the French royal court, carried by trusted messengers to the servants of King Philip IV. Throughout the kingdom of France, royal officers gasped at the orders and sent for their men-at-arms. The predawn hours of Friday, October 13, echoed with the sounds of armed men on the move. Then, precisely at dawn, they struck, pounding on the doors of every chapter house of the Knights Templar in France and arresting everyone inside. Some two thousand members of the order, including a hundred knights and the Grand Master, Jacques de Molay (1244–1314), were seized. The charge was heresy. In 1308, Pope Clement V authorized similar arrests throughout the Christian world.

According to Philip IV's officers, the Templars had abandoned the Christian faith to worship an idol named Baphomet who made plants grow. Scandalous rumors spread, and members of the Templar order were tortured until they confessed to every detail.

Outside of France, investigations found no evidence of wrongdoing, but the French king would accept only one verdict. The order was dissolved by the pope in 1312; outside France, its members were quietly received into other monasteries, and in France, those who confessed to the charges could do the same thing. Those who contested the charges faced a grimmer fate. Fifty-four of them were burned at the stake in 1310; four years later, Grand Master Jacques de Molay and one of his assistants suffered the same fate.

Many historians have argued that Philip IV destroyed the Templars only to get hold of their immense wealth. Among occultists, though, the idea that the Templars had learned occult secrets in the Middle East has been common for centuries, and this belief inspired many later occult groups to take up the Templar heritage.

SEE ALSO: Founding of the Knights Templar (1118)

A miniature from the *Chroniques de France ou de St Denis* (*Chronicles of France or St. Denis*), a history of France composed in a French abbey from c. 1270–1380, originally published in the fourteenth century. It depicts Jacques de Molay, Grand Master of the Templars, and Geoffroi de Charney, the preceptor of Normandy, being burned at the stake in Paris.

A ciaschun tempo in se benignitate
Donno del cielo potencie e uirtute
Che differencia fanno tra le humane
Secondo chel se cerebro te lo mute
Con original quando euer tu in luy
Sença lalteri perfer son uani
Che lanima gen esfaça ben altruy
El como uiue se conosca sole
El como quando mostra certa cole

Caplm. xiij. de la arretia et de illos de patrimonio e du catu :–

O gni crecia cosa uotel tute
Sança la morte che accresa nauara
Che uolta in uso deo le flexure
Per quanto piu possete piu dela
Sar crescose dal ben da la uita amara
El morese la uita mia
uoy del patrimonio e del ducato
Che passo fra alte romani coste
Pur sia pur subiecti al peccato
Mi ma cheme de niete e despouta
Ora poco tempo ue terrino loste
De negra gente col elmi politi
E non prega la crece san francesco
Che guardi assisi delo grifo biancho
Sera spelonca nel deserto fresco
E sa perosa la pena se longa
Sera fenta nello lato mancho

Per lo peccato

CECCO D'ASCOLI BURNED AT THE STAKE

THE CART, SURROUNDED BY A JEERING crowd, hauled the condemned man to an open space where a tall wooden stake had been set up and firewood piled at its foot. Men-at-arms hauled the prisoner from the cart and bound him to the stake. Then, after a few words from the churchmen in attendance, a torch was plunged into the wood, and the condemned man's screams mingled with the roaring of the flames. In medieval Europe, that was the punishment for heresy—but this was the first time this punishment had been meted out for the practice of magic.

Cecco d'Ascoli (1257–1327) became a professor of astronomy and astrology at the University of Bologna in 1322 and wrote a commentary on the *De sphaera* of John of Sacrobosco, the astronomy text used all over Europe at that time. His commentary was full of references to magic and included instructions on summoning a spirit named Floron into a magical statue. Cecco soon found himself hauled in front of the Inquisition.

Condemned as a heretic, he lost his professorship and was barred from teaching; shortly afterward he left Bologna and found a position as court astrologer to the Duke of Florence. Even so powerful a patron, however, could not protect him, and in 1327 he was condemned as a relapsed heretic and sent to the stake.

Cecco's terrible fate was a harbinger of much worse to come, for he was the first person to be condemned as a heretic for magical practices. Until his time, under the guidance of the canon *Episcopi*, the Catholic Church had dismissed the practice of magic as mere superstition, forbidden by church law but punishable only by a minor penance. Heresy, in contrast, was one of the worst crimes under canon law, and once magic was redefined as heresy, the door was open to the violent persecutions of the following centuries.

SEE ALSO: Canon *Episcopi* (9th Century), The Great Valais Witch Trials Begin (1428)

A page from *L'acerba*, a controversial book by Cecco d'Ascoli. *L'acerba* consisted of four finished volumes on subjects including astronomy, the vices and virtues, minerals, and morality, as well as one unfinished volume on theology.

The read Sea the read Sol: the read Elixir vite

Sol Stone
Chris Stone
The white Stone
The Elixir vite

Luna in crescente

THE PHILOSOPHER'S STONE

ROM ANCIENT TIMES UNTIL THE BEGIN-ning of the modern era, there were those who claimed to have accomplished the Great Work of alchemy and created the Philosopher's Stone. Among them were Nicholas (c. 1330–1418) and Perenelle (c. 1320–1397) Flamel. Though they had a minor role in the first of J. K. Rowling's *Harry Potter* novels, the Flamels actually existed, and Nicholas Flamel's account of his travels and labors has been famous since its publication in the early fifteenth century.

Flamel was a professional scribe who collected old books. One day he bought a curious manuscript twenty-one pages long that displayed alchemical emblems with no explanation. He and his wife, Perenelle, who was as interested in alchemy as he was, spent years trying to decipher them. Finally, with Perenelle's blessing, Nicholas went to Spain in the hope of finding an alchemist who could teach him what he needed to know.

There he met an old Jewish alchemist named Canches, who recognized the emblems and agreed to explain them. They set out on the return trip to Paris, but on the way Canches fell ill and died. He had taught Flamel enough, though, that after three years Nicholas and Perenelle made the mysterious First Matter, and the other steps followed soon thereafter. As the legend goes, on January 17, 1382, they succeeded in creating the White Stone and turned half a pound of base metal into pure silver. On April 25 of that year, about five o'clock in the evening, they created the Red Stone and turned half a pound of base metal into pure gold.

Historians agree that Nicholas and Perenelle Flamel existed and became very rich in their later years. The source of their wealth has been the subject of much speculation—but the book of diagrams, which was published along with Flamel's account, remains a core resource for contemporary alchemists.

SEE ALSO: The Fulcanelli Enigma (1926)

An illustration from *The Ripley Scroll,* an alchemical manuscript originally published in the sixteenth century in England. The illustrations use pictorial cryptograms to show the processes for creating the Philosopher's Stone. Nicholas and Perenelle Flamel were among the alchemists who claimed to accomplish this prized feat.

DIANA

VII.

BACCO

VIII.

MERCURIO

IX.

CERES

XII.

ORIGIN OF THE TAROT

PLAYING CARDS REACHED EUROPE FROM the Muslim world in the fourteenth century, but the first decks known in the Western world were like modern playing cards, with four numbered suits. It was in the first years of the fifteenth century that someone thought to add a set of symbolic cards to the pack and create the first Tarot deck. His name was Marziano da Tortona, the personal secretary of Filippo Maria Visconti, Duke of Milan, and an essay about the new cards that he wrote for the duke in 1418 still survives.

The additional cards in Marziano's new deck weren't the same as the standard Tarot sequence. They were ancient Greek deities, sixteen of them, meant to represent virtues and vices. His invention, though, inspired others to make new decks with symbols of their own choosing. Since the sequence of emblems resembled nothing so much as the floats in the grand parades that were a common event in Renaissance Italy, the name of those parades—*Trionfi,* or "triumphs," after the triumphal processions of ancient Rome—came to be used for the symbolic cards. Tarot readers today still call them "trumps."

By 1450 or so, card players in Milan had settled on the twenty-two trumps used today, and cards painted around that year are recognizable forerunners of the modern Tarot deck. Other Italian cities developed similar decks, but it was the Milanese deck that traveled with merchants to Marseilles in France, which would become the most important center of Tarot manufacture. By the early 1800s Tarot had become a common card game all over France, Switzerland, and northern Italy, as common as poker in the United States today. Only in a few places was it used for fortune-telling, though, and it would take a pair of French occultists to transform it into the most important divination system in modern occultism.

SEE ALSO: Tracing the Tarot to Egypt (1781), Etteilla Publicizes Tarot Divination (1783), The Rider-Waite Tarot Deck (1910)

A 2015 re-creation of the Marziano tarot deck by Robert M. Place, depicting ancient deities Diana, Bacchus, Mercury, and Ceres.

Des vaudoises

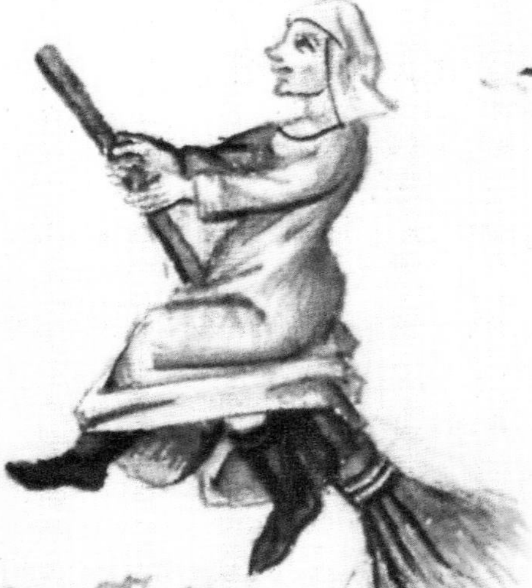

Pisse martin

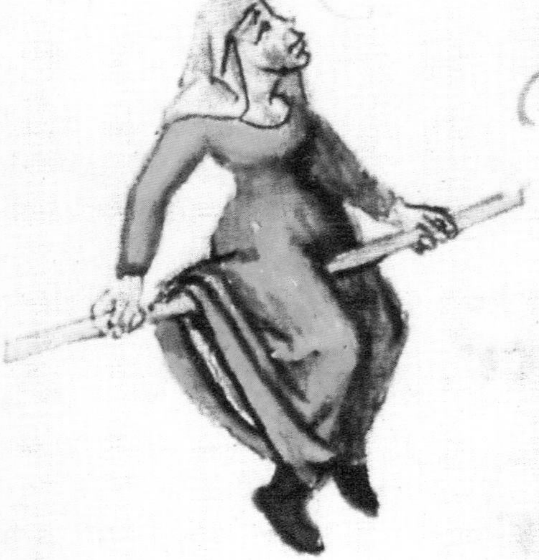

aduers
Respon
Quant tu a
Vray est ouy
Que les vie
Ne vingt m
Vont ensemb
Veoir leurs
Ce nest pas
Tarhe nai
Ne aude pas
En parlant
Quant tu s
Toutes les
Et nest au
Qui leur fa
Le teps auo

THE GREAT VALAIS WITCH TRIALS BEGIN

THE RUMORS HAD BEEN SPREADING FOR months, perhaps years, in Valais in the southern part of Switzerland. Witches were everywhere, people claimed: flying through the air, becoming invisible by means of sinister herbs, turning themselves into wolves to prey on cattle, casting curses on good Christians, and consorting with the Devil. On August 7, 1428, peasants from seven Valais districts went to the authorities and demanded that something be done about it.

The local political and religious officials were more than ready to take action and began rounding up suspects at once. Anyone who was accused of witchcraft by at least three witnesses was arrested. Those who confessed were burned at the stake; those who refused to confess were tortured until they said what their accusers wanted to hear and then were burned. Clerk of the court Johannes Fründ, the author of the most detailed record of the Valais witch trials, noted with amazement that some of the accused kept insisting on their innocence until they died under torture; like most of the officials involved in the trials, he assumed that every person accused of witchcraft must be guilty.

No count was kept of the number of accused witches who were burned or tortured to death in Valais after 1428, but historians have documented well over three hundred victims. From Valais, the hunt for witches spread through most of Switzerland and from there into France and Germany. Even more significant was the Council of Basel, a church council that met from 1431 to 1437 in the Swiss city of Basel and threw the official sanction of the Catholic Church behind the witch panic. Over the years to come, as a direct result, around half a million people would die horrible deaths. The Burning Times had arrived.

SEE ALSO: Canon *Episcopi* (9th Century), The *Malleus Maleficarum* (1486), Passage of the Witchcraft Act (1736)

Two witches, as depicted in *Le champion des dames (The Defender of Women)*, by fifteenth-century French poet Martin Le Franc.

TRANSLATION OF THE CORPUS HERMETICUM

IN THE SECOND HALF OF THE FIFTEENTH century, the Italian city-state of Florence had the liveliest intellectual scene in Europe. Its ruler, Cosimo de' Medici, set up a Florentine Academy to rival the academies of ancient Greece and picked just the person to head it—the brilliant young scholar Marsilio Ficino (1433–1499). As the academy's first project, Ficino had begun a complete Latin translation of the dialogues of Plato. Then, in 1463, a letter reached Cosimo from one of his agents in Greece.

Ten years earlier, Constantinople had fallen to the Turks, and many cultural and literary treasures had been dumped on the market. Cosimo's agent had found one of those works, a copy of the *Corpus Hermeticum*. In 1463, nobody knew about the ancient habit of assigning authorship of texts to mythical sages, and so as far as Cosimo's agent or anyone else knew, the collection had been penned by the ancient Egyptian sage Hermes Trismegistus himself. Cosimo wrote back at once, authorizing the purchase, and told Ficino that Plato would have to wait—something more important was on its way.

Once the precious manuscript arrived, Ficino needed only a few months to translate it into Latin. Copies of the translation circulated widely, first in manuscript and then in printed form. Across Europe, people interested in the occult suddenly had access to the soaring spiritual vision of ancient Hermeticism—a vision that gave occultism an honored place. For a century and a half, until the real date of the *Corpus Hermeticum* became known, the belief in its Egyptian roots gave Hermeticism a prestige it would not otherwise have had and turned it into an immense cultural force across Renaissance Europe.

SEE ALSO: The *Corpus Hermeticum* (3rd Century)

An engraving of Marsilio Ficino by French illustrator Esme de Boulonois, 1682, after Dutch engraver Philip Galle.

MALLEVS

MALEFICARVM.
IN TRES DIVISVS
PARTES,

In quibus {
Concurrentia ad maleficia,
Maleficiorum effectus,
Remedia aduersus maleficia,
}

Et modus procedendi, ac puniendi maleficos abundè con
tinetur, præcipuè autem omnibus Inquisitoribus, & di
uini uerb: concionatoribus utilis, ac necessarius.

Auctore R. P. F. IACOBO SPRENGER
Ordinis Prædicatorum, olim Inquisitore clariss.

Hac postrema editione per F. Raffaelem Masseum Vene-
tum. D. Iacobi a Iudeca instituti Seruorum, summo stu
dio illustratus, & à multis erroribus uindicatus.

His adieci mus indices rerum memorabilium, & quæstionum.

VIRTVTI SIC — CEDIT, INVIDIA:

VENETIIS,
Ad Candentis Salamandræ insigne.
M D LXXVI.

THE MALLEUS MALEFICARUM

HEINRICH KRAMER (C. 1430–C. 1505) AND Jakob Sprenger (c. 1435–1495) were Dominican friars and, like many members of their order in the fifteenth and sixteenth centuries, took an active role in the Inquisition. Their main job was catching and burning witches, and in the early 1480s they set out to write a manual for the benefit of their less experienced colleagues

The identification of magic with heresy that claimed Cecco d'Ascoli as its first victim had become widespread by the time Kramer and Sprenger set pen to paper. To the two inquisitors and to many other church officials, witchcraft was the ultimate heresy, a terrifying threat to Christian society that had to be stamped out with the utmost rigor.

From the first great outbreak of witch hunting in the Valais, inquisitors had pieced together what they thought was an accurate account of witchcraft. When someone was accused of witchcraft, the standard practice of the Inquisition in Germany and some other parts of Europe was straightforward: the accused was read a list of questions—When did you sell your soul to the Devil? How often did you attend the witches' Sabbath? Who else did you see there?—and tortured until he or she gave the answers that the inquisitors expected.

That procedure was enshrined in the pages of Kramer and Sprenger's book, the *Malleus maleficarum* (*Hammer of Witches*), which went on to become the most widely used witch hunter's handbook in early modern Europe. Guided by it or by any of scores of other manuals that embraced the same lethal illogic, witch hunters across Europe tortured and killed tens of thousands of people. Before the Burning Times were over, the persecutions had affected every European country and leaped across the Atlantic to the American colonies, where the Salem witch trials of 1692–1693 were merely the most famous of a series of persecutions that were carried out to combat a threat that never existed.

SEE ALSO: Cecco d'Ascoli Burned at the Stake (1327), The Great Valais Witch Trials Begin (1428)

A page from the *Malleus maleficarum* (*Hammer of Witches*), detailing the three parts of the witch-hunter's guide, including the nature of witches, their powers, and how to persecute them.

EPISTOLÆ
OBSCURORUM
VIRORUM
AD
Dn. M. ORTUINUM
GRATIUM.

Nova & accurata Editio.

Cui quæ accessere, sequens Conten-
torum indicat tabella.

FRANCOFURTI
AD MÆNUM.
ANNO M DC XLIII.

JOHANNES REUCHLIN'S ON THE MIRACULOUS WORD

IN THE BEGINNING, THE CABALA HAD BEEN A wholly Jewish tradition, and it was not until the end of the fifteenth century that a Christian tradition of Cabala began to emerge. Johannes Reuchlin (1455–1522), who set that process in motion, was one of the great scholars of Renaissance Germany. He was fluent in Latin, Greek, and Hebrew, and he studied the Cabala under several Jewish teachers. Convinced that the Cabala was as suitable for Christian mystics as it was for their Jewish equivalents, he wrote a treatise, *De verbo mirifico* (*On the Miraculous Word*), to prove the divinity of Jesus by using Cabalistic methods. Its publication in 1494 inspired many other Christians to study the Cabala.

The backlash was not long in coming. In 1509 a group of Catholic inquisitors petitioned Emperor Maximilian to order all Jewish books except the Old Testament burned. Maximilian consulted Reuchlin and on his advice rejected the petition. The inquisitors retaliated by accusing Reuchlin of heresy. Reuchlin's friends rallied to his support, and after seven years of bitter controversy, Reuchlin triumphed. The pope ordered all proceedings against him dismissed, and Reuchlin's friends unleashed one of history's most influential satires, *Epistolae obscuriorum virorum* (*Letters from Very Obscure Men*), which lampooned Reuchlin's enemies mercilessly and made them laughingstocks across Europe.

While the controversy raged, Reuchlin wrote the first comprehensive treatise on Christian Cabala, *De arte cabalistica* (*On the Cabalistic Art*), which was published in 1517. Reuchlin's prestige as a scholar and the wickedly funny jabs the authors of *Letters from Very Obscure Men* leveled at his opponents helped keep attacks on Christian Cabalists at bay for close to a century.

SEE ALSO: Origins of the Cabala (c. 1230), Abraham Abulafia Goes to Saronno (1279), Isaac Luria Arrives in Safed (1570)

Title page from *Epistolae obscuriorum virorum* (*Letters from Very Obscure Men*), published in 1515 by Reuchlin's friends to satirize his enemies.

PARACELSUS COMES TO BASEL

A DOCTOR'S SON FROM A REMOTE SWISS village, Philippus Aureolus Theophrastus Bombastus Paracelsus von Hohenheim (1493–1541)—Paracelsus for short—studied alchemy and mineralogy in the miner's school in Villach and then pursued a medical degree at Vienna and Ferrara before finding a series of jobs as military surgeon in an assortment of European armies. His wanderings led him through Europe and beyond, to Central Asia and Egypt, and wherever he went, he learned everything he could from local healers and folk magicians.

His great skill as a healer won him an appointment as a professor of medicine at Basel in 1526, but he didn't keep the job long. He drank heavily, enlivened his lectures by publicly burning the works of medical authorities, and got into endless quarrels with his fellow professors, the officials of the university, and the city government. By 1528 he had to flee from the city by night and resume his wandering life.

In the years that followed the debacle at Basel, Paracelsus wrote voluminous books on medicine, alchemy, and magic, expounding a complex system of occult philosophy. He argued that alchemy should focus on the creation of medicines rather than the transmutation of metals into gold and silver, and he was the first occultist to classify spirits into four elemental categories: sylphs of air, salamanders of fire, undines of water, and gnomes of earth.

He drank himself to death in 1541, but his books outlived their author. For the next two centuries, until the eclipse of occultism by the scientific revolution, his ideas and teachings were embraced by occultists across Europe, and the revival of alchemy in the twentieth century drew extensively on his writings.

SEE ALSO: The Modern Alchemical Revival (1960)

Ondine, **by John William Waterhouse** (1849–1917), exhibited in 1872 at the Society of British Artists. Paracelsus divided spirits into four elemental categories, including undines of water, which inspired the water nymphs of later artists and poets.

HENRICUS CORNELIUS AGRIPPA Med & IC EQU

Nascitur Colon
Agrip. 1486
Obijt Anno 1538.

CORNELIUS AGRIPPA'S *THREE BOOKS OF OCCULT PHILOSOPHY*

THERE WERE PLENTY OF FOOTLOOSE scholars roaming across Europe in the Renaissance, and Heinrich Cornelius Agrippa (1486–1535) was to all appearances just one more of them. Born into a noble but impoverished German family, he took a degree at the University of Cologne and then served in the military for a few years before beginning travels that took him from one end of Europe to another. Wherever he went, friends and patrons were waiting for him, and their interests, like his, focused on the forbidden art of ceremonial magic.

In 1509 and 1510 he settled for a time at Sponheim, staying with the famous occultist Johannes Trithemius (1462–1516), and it was there that he wrote the first draft of *De occulta philosophia libri tres* (*Three Books of Occult Philosophy*). As soon as it was finished, friends of Agrippa's began to circulate handwritten copies. Meanwhile, Agrippa resumed his wanderings, meeting influential occultists wherever he went. His network of connections was so vast that historians have wondered if he might have been the emissary of a secret society of Renaissance magicians that had members all over Europe.

In 1528, he stopped for a while in Antwerp and there revised his massive manuscript for publication. The production challenges were considerable, and it didn't help that an inquisitor, Conrad Köllin of Ulm, declared the book heretical nearly as soon as typesetting began. Despite the difficulties, the *Three Books of Occult Philosophy* appeared in 1533. Other editions followed, as did translations into most European languages. For more than three centuries, it was hard to find anyone in Europe interested in occultism who hadn't studied Agrippa's monumental work.

SEE ALSO: Francis Barrett's *The Magus* (1801)

A sixteenth-century engraving of Heinrich Cornelius Agrippa, author of *De occulta philosophia libri tres* (*Three Books of Occult Philosophy*).

THE *PROPHECIES* OF NOSTRADAMUS

BORN IN A FAMILY OF JEWISH CONVERTS TO Christianity, Michel de Nostredame (1503–1566)—Nostradamus was a Latinization of his family name—attended several universities before taking a degree in medicine at Montpellier. He settled in the French town of Agen and married a local girl, but plague struck the town and she died. He then resumed his wandering life.

In 1547 he settled down again in the small town of Salon la Craux in Provence and met and married a wealthy widow, Anne Ponsart Gemelle. This marriage proved to be much less ill-omened than his first, and they had six children together. Though his medical practice and his wife's money provided a sufficient income, Nostradamus was an ambitious man and decided to turn his talent for divination into an income stream.

Starting in 1551, he began to produce an annual almanac with astrological predictions for the coming year. In 1555, he published the first edition of his magnum opus, *Les prophéties de M. Michel Nostradamus* (*The Prophecies of Mr. Michel Nostradamus*). It contained 350 quatrains, or four-line verses, that revealed the secrets of the future. More editions followed; the last one, with a thousand quatrains, appeared two years after his death.

The quatrains are remarkably obscure, written in a confusing style and full of words borrowed from other languages. Some of them appear to predict events that happened centuries after Nostradamus's time; some are so obscure that nobody has been able to figure out what they mean; and still others didn't pan out—the Great King of Terror who was supposed to arrive in 1999, for example, was a no-show. Even so, the predictions of Nostradamus went on to become the most famous set of occult prophecies in the Western world.

SEE ALSO: Merlin and the Battle of Arderydd (573)

The Great Fire of London, with Ludgate and Old St. Paul's, by an anonymous artist, c. 1670, at the Yale Center for British Art. Many believe that Nostradamus correctly predicted the Great Fire of London in 1666.

JOHN DEE SCHEDULES
A ROYAL CORONATION

THE DEATH OF QUEEN MARY I OF ENGLAND, the Catholic ruler of a mostly Protestant nation, brought sighs of relief to many of her subjects, but few were as heartfelt as the one uttered by John Dee. The son of a minor official in Henry VIII's court, Dee (1527–1608) was educated at Cambridge and Louvain and was an expert astrologer as well as a specialist in navigation and geography. From 1551 on, he worked as a consultant to England's burgeoning merchant fleet, but he landed in jail in 1555, accused of casting spells for the benefit of Mary's half sister, Princess Elizabeth. Although all the charges eventually were dismissed, Dee had to walk carefully while Mary lived.

Her death in 1558 changed things completely. Soon a messenger arrived from Elizabeth, asking a very special favor: Could he use his astrological skills to calculate a time for her coronation?

The art of choosing auspicious times for important events, which was called electional astrology, was an important part of the astrologer's tool kit, and Dee responded with alacrity. The coronation took place on January 15, 1559, and astrologers point out that the extraordinary success of Elizabeth's reign offers some evidence for the effectiveness of Dee's calculations. For the next quarter century, Dee was among the leading intellectuals of Elizabethan England, the author of important works on navigation and geometry, as well as a major figure in the secretive Elizabethan occult scene and the author of enigmatic magical texts such as the *Monas hieroglyphica*, which fused alchemy and mysticism.

Elizabeth's patronage was never lavish, though, and Dee and his occult assistant Edward Kelly went to Europe in search of royal patronage. Dee returned to England to a troubled old age. His house at Mortlake had been looted by a mob, Elizabeth was old, and her court had a short memory. He lived in poverty until his death in 1608.

SEE ALSO: Casting Spells for the Pope (1628), Evangeline Adams Acquitted of Fortune-Telling (1914)

John Dee Performing an Experiment before Queen Elizabeth I, oil painting by Henry Gillard Glindoni (1852–1913).

ספר
מעין החכמה

מכתבי הרב האלהי בוצינא קדישא מוהר' **יצחק לוריא** זלה"ה
והוא ספר יקר הערך ולא היה בנמצא אפי' בכתב כ"א מעט מועיר
בעולם ורבים וכן שלימים התאוו תאוה במחיר בלמות דברי
אלהים חיים הנאמרים באמת דבר וגם רלו שיחוקו מילין לבד עילוה
להעלותן על מכבש הדפום וגזרו אומר בהסכמתם כפי אשר יודפס
כל ההסכמות על ספר התמונה :

נדפס פה קק קאָרעץ

תח"ת ממשלת אקונים המיוחם הגדול החסיד החכם יוזיף
טשאַרטערישקי מטאלמיק ליטעווסקי סטאַראַסטי לאָנקי יר"ה

Gedruckt in KORZEC in Volhyni-
en in der Koeniglichen und der Re-
publique privilegirten Druckerey,
Jüdischer Bücher,
von
JOHAÑ ANTHON KRÜGER,
in WARSHCAU.

אין דער פריװילעגירטי דרוקקרייא פון דעם הערן יאהן.
אנטאן קריגער אין װארשוי

בסנת __ גן נעול מעין חתום

ISAAC LURIA ARRIVES IN SAFED

BORN IN JERUSALEM TO A JEWISH FAMILY of German origins, Isaac Luria (1534–1572) was a child prodigy who was respected as a scholar of the Talmud at the age of eight. He was orphaned while still a child and went to live with relatives in Egypt, where he studied with some of the leading rabbis of his era. At that time, most teachers of the Cabala would not take students under the age of forty; Luria's scholarship was such that he was introduced to it at age seventeen. He devoted the next fifteen years of his life to the Cabala, culminating with two years of intensive meditation in a hut on the banks of the Nile.

At the conclusion of those two years, in 1570, a vision commanded him to return to the Holy Land. At that time the city of Safed was the most influential center of Cabalistic studies, and there Luria went. His lectures in Safed quickly attracted disciples, some of whom were already famous Cabalists. To them he expounded an extraordinary teaching that reframed Cabalistic tradition into a grand narrative of fall and redemption.

One of the great challenges faced by devout Jews as well as believers in other faiths is the problem of evil: If God is benevolent and almighty, why should there be so much suffering in the world? Luria's answer was that the forces that cause suffering and evil in the world are remnants of the universe before ours—a primal cosmos of unbalanced forces—and the mission of human beings, and Jews in particular, is to redeem the powers of evil through religious observance and Cabalistic disciplines.

Luria died after a short illness just two years after his arrival in Safed, but his teachings became the foundation on which most later Cabalists built. As the Cabala was adopted by occultists across Europe, Luria's ideas became a potent influence on the entire occult tradition.

SEE ALSO: Origins of the Cabala (c. 1230), Abraham Abulafia Goes to Saronno (1279), Johannes Reuchlin's *On the Miraculous Word* (1494)

The Mayan ha-hokhmah, or *Fountain of Wisdom,* pictured here, was a seventeenth-century introduction to the Cabala, attributed to R. Asher Jacob Abraham ben Aryeh Leib Kalmankes (d. 1681), largely drawn from the works of Isaac Luria.

THE *BENANDANTI*

HE INQUISITORS OF FRIULI IN THE NORTH-eastern corner of Italy were completely baffled. Hearing reports of a heretical cult in the Friulian countryside, they brought in peasants for questioning, but the answers they got didn't sound like any heresy they had encountered before. It wasn't the witchcraft discussed in the *Malleus maleficarum*, or the old Catharism, or the new Lutheran heresy that was causing trouble in Germany. What could it be?

The Friulian Inquisition had stumbled upon the *benandanti*, a strange agrarian cult of unknown origins. The *benandanti*—the name means "good walkers"—had all been born with a caul, that is, a piece of the amniotic membrane, on their heads. According to their beliefs, on certain days each year, as they slept, they left their bodies and traveled in animal form to a valley at the center of the world, where they did battle with sinister sorcerers called *malandanti*, "evil walkers." If the *benandanti* won, the harvest would be good; if their opponents triumphed, bad

weather would ruin the crops. *Benandanti* also could heal illnesses and cure those who had been bewitched.

The laws governing the Inquisition in Italy, unlike those in most other parts of Europe, did not permit the use of torture. As a result, where a French or German inquisitor would have tortured the prisoners until they confessed to witchcraft or heresy, the Friulian inquisitors were forced to take the testimony of their prisoners seriously. Though they brought in more than a hundred *benandanti* for questioning between 1575 and 1644, very few were put to death; most were sent home and told not to believe such superstitions in the future. The records of the Friulian Inquisition thus contain one of the few detailed accounts of a tradition related to the one discussed in the canon *Episcopi* more than six hundred years earlier.

SEE ALSO: Canon *Episcopi* (9th Century), The *Malleus Maleficarum* (1486)

The Witches' Sabbath, a woodcut by Hans Baldung, 1510. The *benandanti* claimed to protect their harvest by traveling outside their bodies to battle malevolent witches during their sabbath.

THE LEGEND OF FAUST

THE PRINTING PRESS WAS THE INTERNET OF early modern Europe, a hot new communications technology that made information more readily available than it had ever been before, and the pamphlets and books that streamed out of early European presses were as diverse in quality as blogs and social media are today. Most of that output vanished without a trace, but some had a lasting impact; Johann Spies's *Geschichte der Doktor Johannes Fausten* (*History of Dr. Johannes Fausten*) was one of the latter.

Spies (c. 1540–c. 1623) collected an assortment of legends about people who sold their souls to the Devil and applied them to Johannes Faustus (c. 1480–c. 1540), a minor German occultist who died half a century before the book saw print. The *History* became a European bestseller and was translated into many languages. Two years after Spies's book was published, the great English playwright Christopher Marlowe wrote a play based on it, *The Tragicall History of Doctor Faustus*. Over the years that followed, the Faust story inspired everything from puppet plays and a grand opera by Charles Gounod to one of the great works of German literature, Johann Wolfgang von Goethe's *Faust*.

Ironically, the popularity of the Faust legend—in which Faust sells his soul to the Devil in exchange for power and wealth and is dragged off to hell after a fixed number of years—inspired an entire literature of magical handbooks instructing would-be sorcerers on the best way to summon demons and get them to fork over cold, hard cash. As with most later systems of "prosperity magic," the only people who succeeded in conjuring up fortunes by means of those books were their authors and publishers. In the process, though, the Faust literature succeeded in giving new life to the hackneyed claim that occultists worship the Christian Devil.

SEE ALSO: Founding of the Hellfire Club (1746)

Faust and Gretchen, painted by Pedro Américo (1843–1905) in the nineteenth century. In the play by Johann Wolfgang von Goethe, Faust uses the devil's influence to seduce Gretchen.

GIORDANO BRUNO
BURNED AT THE STAKE

HERE WOULD BE NO CHANCE OF ESCAPE this time. The renegade friar was hauled in chains to the Campo de' Fiori outside the gates of Rome, where a stake had been set up and wood piled around it. The soldiers of the pope tied him to the stake; after a few formalities, one of them threw a lit torch onto the pyre, and the cries of the doomed man blended with the roaring of the flames and the catcalls of the crowd.

Thus died Giordano Bruno (1548–1600), one of the most colorful figures in Renaissance occultism. He became a Dominican friar at the age of fifteen and showed promise as a scholar. When he was caught reading books on magic, though, he had to flee Italy with the Inquisition hot on his heels.

For the next seventeen years he wandered around Europe, writing and teaching. Among the Dominicans, he had learned the Art of Memory, a system of memory training dating from ancient Greece, and many of his books expounded forms of that system, mixed with magical imagery and Hermetic philosophy. All through his wanderings he hoped to find an aristocratic patron. When a Venetian nobleman named Zuan Mocenigo contacted him in 1591, Bruno thought he had hit the jackpot and made the fatal mistake of returning to Italy. Mocenigo betrayed him to the Inquisition, and after eight years in a dungeon in Rome, he was burned at the stake as a heretic.

Ironically, once he was safely dead, Bruno was redefined as a martyr for science. For centuries, historians quietly ignored the vast amount of occultism in his writing and insisted that he had been burned at the stake for his belief that the earth circled the sun and there were an infinite number of habitable worlds in space. Only in the middle years of the twentieth century, when scholarly prejudices against occultism had begun to fade, did the scope and depth of his occult involvements become clear.

SEE ALSO: Cecco d'Ascoli Burned at the Stake (1327)

Condemnation of Giordano Bruno, who was burned at the stake, in this relief by Ettore Ferrari, on the base of the monument to Giordano Bruno (1889), in Campo de' Fiori square in Rome, Italy.

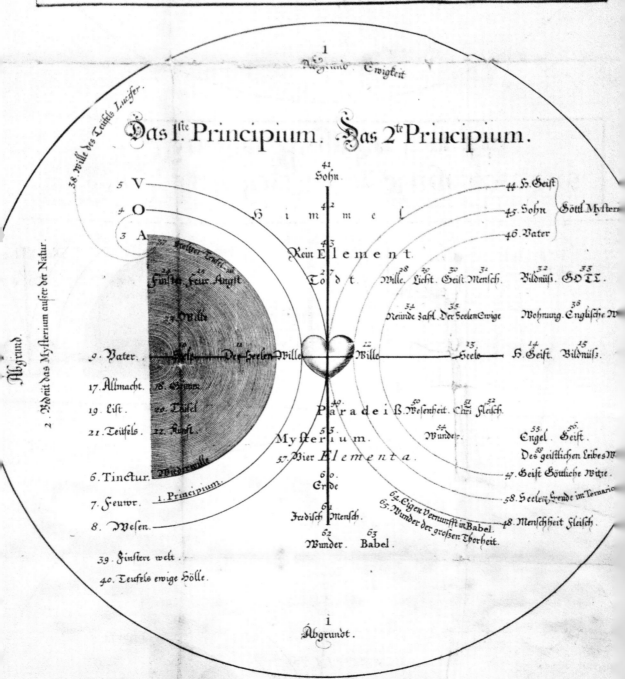

THE VISIONS OF JACOB BOEHME

JACOB BOEHME (1575–1624) WAS A SHOE-maker in the modest German town of Goerlitz, a churchgoing Lutheran married to the local butcher's daughter: hardly the sort of man to whom mystical visions came naturally. As he approached middle age, though, he began studying the writings of Paracelsus and other alchemists. His studies resulted around 1610 in a tremendous vision in which he saw the secret "signatures" in all things. The attempt to express his vision in words gave rise to his first book, *Aurora, oder die Morgenroete im Aufgang* (*Aurora, or the Dawn and Beginning*), which circulated in manuscript and attracted to Boehme a circle of mystically inclined friends.

The local Lutheran pastor denounced the book as heretical and forbade Boehme to write anything further. Boehme tried to obey the injunction, but the pressure of his vision was too great, and he took to writing in secret, turning out essays on mystical and alchemical Christianity. Copies were passed around secretly among Boehme's friends, who saw to it that the shoemaker-mystic had access to the latest alchemical literature. Eventually his writings attracted enough interest from politically influential scholars that the Lutheran church's ban was lifted and several of his books were published.

After Boehme's death in 1624, the rest of his writings quickly saw print and became immensely influential in the rise of Christian occultism. Nearly all the significant figures in this tradition drew extensively from Boehme's ideas, and one of the major initiatory traditions of modern occultism—the Martinist tradition—derives a great deal of its teachings from Boehme by way of the shoemaker's influence on Louis-Claude de Saint-Martin and his followers.

SEE ALSO: Paracelsus Comes to Basel (1526), The Martinist Order (1884)

A drawing of Jacob Boehme's cosmogony in *Vierzig Fragen von der Seele*, or *Forty Questions of the Soul* (1620).

INTREPIDO SIS CORD

S SVPERES AQVILA

FACIE IVVENIS

ACCALCE TERENS BOS

1 6 2 7

FECIT MICHI MAGNALIA QVI POTENS EST .
ET SANCTVM SANCTVM SANCTV NOMĒ EIVS

JOHANNES BUREUS
INTERPRETS THE RUNES

ALL OVER THE SWEDISH COUNTRYSIDE, standing stones marked with odd angular letters bear witness to the pre-Christian past. For centuries, few people paid attention to them, but by the late sixteenth century, in Sweden as elsewhere, people stopped treating the Bible as an accurate account of history. That was when a young man named Johannes Bureus (1568–1652) began roaming Sweden and copying the runic inscriptions he found.

At first this was a scholarly hobby, but friends in the Swedish government soon saw to it that he received a salary. By 1600 he could read the inscriptions. He became convinced as he studied the runes that there was a deeper secret buried in the inscriptions, and like so many scholars of his time, he turned to occultism to help unearth that secret.

After close study of the Cabala and John Dee's mysterious book *Monas hiero-glyphica*, Bureus was convinced that he knew the mystery hidden within the runes:

the Adulruna, the template from which the runic alphabet derived, which fused symbolism with Pythagorean geometry and also provided a key to the prophecies of the Bible. In 1611 he wrote a first draft of his findings, titled *Adulruna rediviva* (*Adulruna Renewed*), and presented a copy to Gustavus Adolphus, the newly crowned king of Sweden. More than thirty years later, in 1643, Bureus's final edition was presented to Queen Christina, Gustavus Adophus's daughter, but neither monarch could make heads or tails of it.

After Bureus's death in 1652, his work was taken up by younger students who built on the historical and linguistic side of his work and ignored the occult dimension. By then the Age of Reason was dawning, and occultism faced two more centuries of exile.

SEE ALSO: Invention of the Runes (1st Century CE), Guido von List's Vision of the Runes (1902), Ralph Blum's *The Book of Runes* (1983)

Johannes Bureus depicted on a 1627 painting signed "J. L.," Gripsholm Castle, Sweden.

JOHANNES BUREUS
INTERPRETS THE RUNES

LL OVER THE SWEDISH COUNTRYSIDE, standing stones marked with odd angular letters bear witness to the pre-Christian past. For centuries, few people paid attention to them, but by the late sixteenth century, in Sweden as elsewhere, people stopped treating the Bible as an accurate account of history. That was when a young man named Johannes Bureus (1568–1652) began roaming Sweden and copying the runic inscriptions he found.

At first this was a scholarly hobby, but friends in the Swedish government soon saw to it that he received a salary. By 1600 he could read the inscriptions. He became convinced as he studied the runes that there was a deeper secret buried in the inscriptions, and like so many scholars of his time, he turned to occultism to help unearth that secret.

After close study of the Cabala and John Dee's mysterious book *Monas hiero-glyphica*, Bureus was convinced that he knew the mystery hidden within the runes:

the Adulruna, the template from which the runic alphabet derived, which fused symbolism with Pythagorean geometry and also provided a key to the prophecies of the Bible. In 1611 he wrote a first draft of his findings, titled *Adulruna rediviva* (*Adulruna Renewed*), and presented a copy to Gustavus Adolphus, the newly crowned king of Sweden. More than thirty years later, in 1643, Bureus's final edition was presented to Queen Christina, Gustavus Adolphus's daughter, but neither monarch could make heads or tails of it.

After Bureus's death in 1652, his work was taken up by younger students who built on the historical and linguistic side of his work and ignored the occult dimension. By then the Age of Reason was dawning, and occultism faced two more centuries of exile.

SEE ALSO: Invention of the Runes (1st Century CE), Guido von List's Vision of the Runes (1902), Ralph Blum's *The Book of Runes* (1983)

1611

Johannes Bureus depicted on a 1627 painting signed "J. L.," Gripsholm Castle, Sweden.

DAT ROSA MEL APIBUS

THE FIRST ROSICRUCIAN MANIFESTO

IN THE EARLY SEVENTEENTH CENTURY, THE printer Wilhelm Wessel of Cassel in Germany brought out an anonymous pamphlet titled *Fama Fraternitatis* (*Announcement of the Fraternity*). According to that document, a secret society called the Fraternity of the Rosy Cross had been founded by the sage Christian Rosenkreutz. After Rosenkreutz's death in 1484, he and the occult secrets of the fraternity had been hidden away in a secret vault. The vault had been rediscovered in 1604, and the fraternity was seeking new members.

The publication of the *Fama* launched an extraordinary furor. Across Europe, people tried to find the fraternity—some to join it, others to burn its members at the stake. Another manifesto, the *Confessio Fraternitatis* (*Confession of the Fraternity*), followed in 1615, and 1616 saw the publication of *The Chemical Wedding of Christian Rosenkreutz*, a strange alchemical tale supposedly written by the founder of the fraternity. Dozens of other books, pamphlets, and broadsheets appeared, praising the fraternity, condemning it, questioning its existence, and claiming to offer its secret wisdom. To use a modern phrase, the fraternity had gone viral.

Who wrote the manifestos? The evidence points to a circle of intellectuals at the University of Tübingen in Germany, and there is reason to think they wrote the *Fama* as a deliberate hoax, a learned joke of a kind highly popular in Europe at that time. Whatever their original intentions, their creation took on a life of its own, and within a few decades occultists who identified themselves as Rosicrucians—from the Latin *rosae crucis*, "of the rose and cross"—could be found across much of Europe.

SEE ALSO: Rosicrucians Arrive in Pennsylvania (1694), The "Wars of the Roses" (1925)

The iconic rose and cross appear on the title page of *Summum bonum* (1629), a defense of Rosicrucianism by British cosmologist Robert Fludd, writing as Joachim Frizius.

VRBANVS VIII. PONTIFEX MAX.
Romæ Creatus anno M.D.CXXIII
Die VI. Augusti.

CASTING SPELLS FOR THE POPE

OLD TERROR MUST HAVE PASSED through the renegade friar when the messengers of the pope arrived at his humble dwelling in Rome. Tommaso Campanella (1568–1639) had every reason to fear the power of the Catholic Church; he had been imprisoned twice for heresy and a third time for leading a rebellion against Spanish rule in southern Italy, a rising in which Campanella's occultism played a central role. While in prison the third time, he had written a utopian book, *Civitas solis* (*The City of the Sun*), in which he expounded a vision of a perfect society governed by astrological magic.

None of this was likely to endear him to the church hierarchy, and Campanella knew it. In fact, the current pope, Urban VIII, had issued a papal bull forbidding astrology. The messengers assured Campanella, however, that they were not there to haul him before a tribunal. Instead, they wanted him to do a very special favor for the pope.

Urban's opposition to astrology, it turned out, was a facade. He was himself an astrologer, and he feared that an approaching eclipse in a baleful relationship to his birth chart would bring about his death. He wanted Campanella to perform rituals to ward off the effects of the eclipse. This Campanella was more than willing to do. Following the teachings of *Picatrix* and the *Corpus Hermeticum*, he prepared a chamber with magical images invoking beneficent planets, and he and the pope together burned incense and recited incantations for days on end until the malefic influence of the eclipse was safely past.

The ritual seems to have worked—Pope Urban VIII lived for another sixteen years, dying at the healthy old age of seventy-six—and Campanella lived the rest of his life free from any threat from the Inquisition.

SEE ALSO: The *Corpus Hermeticum* (3rd Century), Translation of *Picatrix* (1256), John Dee Schedules a Royal Coronation (1559)

1628

A seventeenth-century engraving of Pope Urban VIII by Matthäus Merian the Elder (1593–1650).

N.° 13.   N.° 12.   N.° II.   N.° 10.   N.° 9.   N.°

Circulus   N.° 5.   Circulus   N.° 1.   Tabula XII.   Circulus

GERARD THIBAULT'S ACADEMY OF THE SWORD

T HE RENAISSANCE REVIVAL OF OCCULTISM wasn't limited to magic, astrology, and alchemy; the geometry of Pythagoras also received new attention. Renaissance artists and architects drew on it, and so did Renaissance swordsmen. Fencers took up geometry to refine their technique, and their new ways of fighting spread across Europe, flourishing especially in Spain.

The swordsman who fused combat and geometry most completely, Gerard Thibault (1574–1629), was born in Antwerp, Belgium. Sickly as a child, he took up fencing to improve his health and traveled to Spain to learn from some of Europe's best teachers. When he came home in 1611, he won a competition against the best swordsmen in Belgium and Holland and then took on all comers in a famous exhibition before Prince Maurice of Nassau and defeated them all.

He then set to work on a manual, *Academie de l'Espée* (*Academy of the Sword*), which saw print a year after his death in 1629. In this, the most elaborate treatise on swordsmanship ever written, he rooted the art of the sword in Pythagorean geometry, quoted Cornelius Agrippa's *Three Books of Occult Philosophy* at length in the introduction, and included two big copperplate engravings packed with occult symbolism. No one reading his book could have mistaken Thibault's art for anything but what it was: a European martial art with deep ties to occultism.

None of this kept Thibault's book from being funded by monarchs and aristocrats, and his method of swordsmanship was practiced in Belgium, Holland, and parts of Germany for many years after his death. The tide already had begun to turn against the occult revival, however. As rationalism grew in popularity, anything associated with occultism dropped out of favor, including Thibault's swordsmanship. Less than a century after his death, he and his work had been forgotten.

SEE ALSO: Pythagoras Comes to Crotona (6th Century BCE), Cornelius Agrippa's *Three Books of Occult Philosophy* (1533)

Plate from Gerard Thibault's *Academie de l'Espée* (*Academy of the Sword*) (1630), depicting defensive postures for a duel involving rapiers used in the Spanish style.

WILLIAM LILLY,
Born April 30. 14 H. 8 m. PM.
1602.

WILLIAM LILLY'S
CHRISTIAN ASTROLOGY

A FARM BOY FROM A POOR NOTTINGHAM-shire family, William Lilly (1602–1681) attended grammar school but could not afford the education of his dreams. Instead, he went to London and worked for a wealthy businessman. Then his employer died, and his elderly widow fell in love with Lilly. The marriage made him wealthy, and when she died a few years later, he sold the business and invested the proceeds in the education he'd always desired.

Astrology was his great interest, and within a few years he was in much demand as an astrologer. In the troubled politics of the time, he took the side of the parliamentarian party against the royalists and began publishing predictions of victory for Parliament and a violent death for King Charles I. His prophecies turned out to be correct: the parliamentary forces triumphed in the English Civil War, and Charles was executed in 1649.

In the middle of this turmoil, Lilly worked on his magnum opus, the first complete textbook of astrology ever published in the English language. Titled *Christian Astrology*, it was published in 1647 and went on to become the standard textbook on the subject for aspiring astrologers, maintaining that status until well into the nineteenth century.

Lilly's decision to write his textbook in English rather than Latin, the ordinary language of scholarship in his time, had immense consequences. Within half a century of the book's publication, the Age of Reason and its rationalist science had seized the imagination of the Western world, and occultism dropped out of fashion. The traditions that survived did so primarily among folk practitioners who knew no Latin. Because astrology was available to anyone literate in English, it survived in the English-speaking world, and it was from there that the astrological revival of the nineteenth century burst onto the scene.

SEE ALSO: The First Horoscopes (Late 5th Century BCE), Dane Rudhyar's *The Astrology of Personality* (1936)

An eighteenth-century copperplate astrological birth chart for William Lilly, as appeared in Ebenezer Sibly's *New and Complete Illustration of the Celestial Science of Astrology.*

PRIMUM MOBILE.

NHOS ꜱꜱꜱ H: GEIST

Omnia
NA — Una
PRIMA — TURA
MATERIA

Das Erschaffene endlich
und der ewigt Gottes Sohn.

Prima Naturabin ich genant,
von Gott den Menschen zum dienst
gesandt.

Einfältig, warhafft, gerecht
und beständig,
Äusserlich groß, und klein
Inwendig.
Noch wollen meine Kinder
mich nicht kennen,
Ob ich mich schon nützlich
 mensch zu nennen.

Primum Mobile Kiel LUX
hebe auf den Wassern

Also muß seyn mein
Laborant
Der Marchandizen will in
meinem Land,
Einfältig, warhafft from
und Gerecht.
sonst wird er mir zum
Feuckers Knecht.
Wer nicht will haben
diesen Nahmen,
Sein mirabbit und
Byrese amen.

Quod est Superius
de Anterius
IGNIS
Luft ☿ Saame
Animalisch Saame

Coelestisch Saame

FIGURA

SUL- MW
PHR MER-
CURI-
US
TU Tin ctur RA
und bre ge ein
Jedes sei nes gleichen

CABBALISTICA

Animalisch Saame
Feuer Erde

AQVA

Vegetabilisch Saame
Mineralisch Saame

Kennst mich
Beschweig stille Jatto
in gesein.

Ergetz sich das AER

Vegetabilisch Saame

Mineralisch Saame

Mein Schatz ver-
birg mach nicht
Gemein.

PLUS — ULTRA

TER-
RA

Ein Prophet gilt
nichts in seinem
Vaterlande......

CHAOS

MITTE
POLUS ARCTI
RNACHT
ARCTICO

CHAOS

Wenn er nicht seine
Liebe bestätigt mit
Wunderwercken.

Ele — menta
Ele — menta
Ele — menta
Ele — menta
Ele — menta
Ele — menta

CHAOS

CHAOS
MOR
GEN

CHAOS

Equinoctium

CHAOS
AB
ENT — ta
ANT — entia
entia
enta
menta

Elementa
Equinoctium
Element
Element
Element

Elementa
Elementa
Element

CHAOS
AB

Unum

Equinoctium

MIT TAG

ROSICRUCIANS ARRIVE IN PENNSYLVANIA

THE LITTLE GROUP OF MEN FILED DOWN the gangplank into the bustle of Philadelphia's harbor district, glad to set foot on land again after the long sea voyage from Germany. Like so many others, they had chosen to leave behind everything they knew to make a new life in the English colonies of North America, but their motives were unusual. Members of a Rosicrucian society called the Chapter of Perfection, they wanted to practice alchemy, astrology, and Cabala without interference from religious authorities, and the colony of Pennsylvania—whose founder, William Penn, had taken the unthinkable step of granting its residents the right to freedom of religion—seemed as full of promise to them as it did to many other religious minorities of that era.

Not long after their arrival, the little band settled on property in what is now Germantown Creek, Pennsylvania. There they built what would now be called a commune, living together in one house and sharing all their property. Working together, the brothers raised all their own food and other necessities of life, and German immigrants in the area turned to them for medical and magical help, as their ancestors in Germany had turned to folk healers and wizards for centuries.

The leader of the group, Johannes Kelpius (1667–1708), died from the severe austerities he practiced, and Conrad Matthai became the new head of the Chapter of Perfection. Under his leadership, the communal structure was dissolved, and the brethren moved into little cabins of their own and pursued their physical and spiritual labors individually. Some became full-time folk healers and magicians for the immigrant communities around them and taught students of their own. Although the Chapter did not outlive its original members, those students passed on much of their lore and helped give rise to the distinctive Pennsylvania tradition of folk magic.

SEE ALSO: The First Rosicrucian Manifesto (1614), The "Wars of the Roses" (1925)

Secret Rosicrucian figures and symbols from the sixteenth and seventeenth centuries, from an early-nineteenth-century manuscript titled *Physica, metaphysica et hyperphysica* (*Physical, Metaphysical, and Hyperphysical*).

THE FIRST MASONIC GRAND LODGE

LIKE EVERY OTHER TAVERN IN EARLY EIGH-teenth-century London, the Apple Tree tavern in London's Covent Garden district had rooms upstairs for private parties and clubs. On the evening of June 24, 1717, none of the patrons who sat in the main room gave a second thought to the men in fashionable wigs who came in through the front door, climbed the stairs, and went to the door of one of the private rooms: a door guarded by a man with a drawn sword.

In medieval Europe, members of every skilled profession belonged to trade organizations called guilds. Few guilds survived the end of the Middle Ages, but the stonemasons' guild in England and Scotland was an exception, and its elaborate symbolism and initiation rituals drew "accepted members"— honorary members, in today's language— from outside the stonemasons' trade. In 1717 there were four stonemasons' lodges in London, and the meeting on June 24 had been called for the purpose of organizing the first Grand Lodge of Masons.

Freemasonry, the philosophical and charitable organization that developed out of the old stonemasons' lodges, was not and is not an occult organization. Masonry's ties to sacred geometry and occult symbolism and the opportunities to network with the like-minded, though, led many occultists to become Masons from the mid-eighteenth to the mid-twentieth century. In fact, if a man was interested in the occult, it was usually a safe bet that he was a Mason as well. As a result, a great deal of Masonic tradition flowed into occultism. In particular, lodges founded and run along Masonic lines, performing initiation rituals modeled on Masonic ceremonies, began to play a significant role in occultism once the tradition entered its great nineteenth-century revival—a process that reached its culmination 170 years later with the foundation of the Hermetic Order of the Golden Dawn.

SEE ALSO: The Élus Coens (1767), The Hermetic Order of the Golden Dawn (1887)

1717

The modern-day Freemasons' Hall, located on Great Queen Street in London, was built between 1927 and 1933. It is the headquarters of the United Grand Lodge of England, the world's oldest Grand Lodge.

A
DISCOURSE
ON
WITCHCRAFT.

Occafioned by a BILL now depending in PAR-
LIAMENT, to repeal the Statute made in the
firft Year of the Reign of King JAMES I, Inti-
tuled, *An Act againft* CONJURATION, WITCH-
CRAFT, *and dealing with evil and wicked*
SPIRITS.

CONTAINING,

Seven CHAPTERS on the following HEADS.

I. To prove that the Bible
has been falfely tranflated in
thofe Places which fpeak of
Witchcraft.

II. That the Opinion of *Witches*,
has had its Foundation in
Heathen Fables.

III. That it hath been im-
proved by the Papal Inqui-
fitors, feeking their own
private Gain, as alfo to efta-
blifh the Ufurped Dominion
of their Founder.

IV. That there is no fuch
Thing as a *Witch* in the
Scriptures, and that there
is no fuch Thing as a *Witch*
at all.

V. An Anfwer to their Arguments who endeavour to
prove there are *Witches.*

VI. How the Opinion of
Witches came at firft into
the World.

VII. The Conclufion.

Nam ut verè loquamur fuperftitio fufa per orbem oppreffit omni-
um ferè animos, atque hominum occupavit imbecillitatem.
                                        Cic. Lib. 2. de Divinat.

LONDON:

Printed for J. READ, in *White-Fryars*; and fold by
the Bookfellers and Pamphlet-Shops of *London* and
Weftminfter, 1736. Price One Shilling.

PASSAGE OF THE WITCHCRAFT ACT

T HE TITLE OF THE NEW STATUTE ECHOED those of previous acts of Parliament: *An Act against Conjuration, Witchcraft, and Dealing with Evil and Wicked Spirits.* But the Witchcraft Act of 1736 completely transformed the legal climate in which British occultists had had to live. It ended witch trials and made it a crime to accuse someone of witchcraft. It also redefined occultism as fraud, stating that those who "pretend to exercise or use any kind of Witchcraft, Sorcery, Enchantment, or Conjuration, or undertake to tell Fortunes" risk a year in prison.

All over Europe, the great tide of persecution was ebbing at last. England saw its last execution for witchcraft in 1682, Scotland in 1722, France in 1745, Germany in 1775, and Switzerland in 1782. People of goodwill throughout the Western world, sickened by the religious wars and witchcraft trials of the seventeenth century, turned away from traditional religious beliefs and embraced the newly minted rationalist philosophies of the Enlightenment. For rationalists, the old laws condemning witchcraft made easy targets for denunciation.

Under the new legislation, people could study occultism without running the risk of a witchcraft trial, and the abolition of press censorship in England in 1695 already had sparked a boom in books and pamphlets on occult lore. In the decades that followed the passage of the Witchcraft Act, that boom expanded to include serious textbooks of occult theory and practice.

A great many occult practices, however, remained illegal, and though the parts of the Witchcraft Act that prohibited magic and fortune-telling were rarely enforced, occultists who were too public about their activities sometimes faced prosecution. Similar laws went on the books in most Western countries and remained in force well into the twentieth century, forcing occultists to remain silent about their activities or risk jail. In 1944, Scottish medium Helen Duncan became the last person imprisoned under the Witchcraft Act, which was finally repealed in 1951.

SEE ALSO: Canon *Episcopi* (9th Century), The *Malleus Maleficarum* (1486)

"A Discourse on Witchcraft," an anonymous text printed in 1736 in response to the Witchcraft Act before Parliament, sold by booksellers and pamphlet shops in London and Westminster.

THE VISIONS OF
EMANUEL SWEDENBORG

EMANUEL SWEDENBORG (1688–1772) WAS not a typical visionary. The son of a Lutheran bishop from a family with close ties to the Swedish throne, he received a first-rate scientific education at Uppsala University in Sweden and followed it with visits to universities and learned societies in England, France, the Netherlands, and Germany. Thereafter he took a government job as an inspector of mines, launched Sweden's first scientific journal, and wrote no fewer than 154 books on the sciences and mathematics.

Swedenborg was in his fifties when his interests turned to occultism, and he began keeping a journal of his dreams and practicing meditation. Those practices bore unexpected fruit in 1744 with an intense visionary experience in which Jesus and the spirit of Swedenborg's dead father appeared to him. This was the first of many visions that convinced Swedenborg that he had a special spiritual mission and set him to work on the first of many books.

He approached his visionary experiences in the same spirit in which he had classified ores for the department of mines: patiently and systematically, comparing the testimony of one set of angels with that of another. His first book on occult subjects, the massive twelve-volume *Arcana coelestia* (*Celestial Secrets*), appeared anonymously in 1749; his authorship soon leaked out, launching a controversy among European intellectuals that endured long after Swedenborg died.

Despite criticism from scientists and condemnation from religious authorities, Swedenborg labored on. By the end of his life he had written more than two hundred books on occult and religious subjects. His writings helped keep interest in occultism alive straight through the Age of Reason and encouraged the growth of the underground occult counterculture from which the great occult revival of the late nineteenth century would burgeon.

SEE ALSO: The Visions of Andrew Jackson Davis (1844)

Portrait of Emanuel Swedenborg, Swedish, by Per Krafft the Elder, c. 1766. The seventy-five-year-old Swedenborg holds the manuscript of his upcoming book, *Apocalypsis revelata (Apocalypse Revealed)*.

FOUNDING OF THE HELLFIRE CLUB

SERIOUS OCCULTISTS WEREN'T THE ONLY ones to benefit from the passage of the Witchcraft Act. Ten years after Parliament passed it, Sir Francis Dashwood (1708–1781) and a coterie of friends founded a society to act out their taste for drunken orgies and medieval kitsch. In 1746 a craze for all things Gothic was becoming a major presence in English pop culture, and ghosts, curses, monks, and the like, were fashionable; thus, it was no surprise when Dashwood fixed up a ruined abbey near Medmenham for the group. Its official name was the Order of the Friars of St. Francis of Wycombe; the name by which it is best known today is the Hellfire Club.

The club's motto was *Fais ce que tu voudras*—"Do what thou wilt" in French. Members wore hooded robes and participated in burlesque Satanic rituals, but their primary activities involved a great deal of alcohol and plenty of indiscriminate sex. The club had one of eighteenth-century England's best collections of pornography along with a steady supply of "nuns" who were either professional sex workers hired for the purpose or enthusiastic amateurs who wanted to step outside the rigid proprieties of upper-class English society. With such entertainments on hand, the club became highly popular, attracting leading politicians and aristocrats, including such major figures as John Wilkes and Benjamin Franklin.

Before the repeal of the old laws against witchcraft, none of this would have been possible, and as it was, the Hellfire Club collapsed in a cloud of scandal in the 1760s. During and after its life-span, however, it played an important role in spreading the idea that occultism had something to do with the rejection of conventional social and sexual mores. Over the next two centuries, that belief had a significant impact on occultism itself.

SEE ALSO: Passage of the Witchcraft Act (1736)

Sir Francis Dashwood (Lord Le Despenser) at His Devotions, a satirical engraving parodying Renaissance images of Francis of Assisi, c. 1760, formerly attributed to William Hogarth; now thought to be by William Platt.

Depasqually de latour

1722 - 1774

THE ÉLUS COENS

TO THIS DAY HE REMAINS A MYSTERIOUS figure. Martinez de Pasqually (c. 1727–1774) probably was born in the town of Grenoble, the child of a Spanish father and a French mother, and there were rumors that he had Jewish ancestry. No one knows where he gained his prodigious knowledge of occultism or where he was initiated into Freemasonry.

All that is known for certain is that he showed up in Montpellier in 1754 and founded a Masonic lodge there that conferred degrees full of occult lore. Over the next twelve years he traveled across France, initiating students and founding new lodges. In 1766, he went to Paris in the hope of getting approval for his lodges from the French Grand Lodge, but that organization dissolved in December of that year after a fight broke out in the middle of a meeting.

Martinez de Pasqually's trip was far from fruitless, though, for in Paris he met Jean-Baptiste Willermoz (1730–1824), a Freemason from Lyons. The next year, the two of them founded *La Franc-Maçonnerie des Chevaliers Maçons Élus Coëns de l'Univers* (Freemasonry of the Knight Masons, Chosen Priests of the Universe), *Élus Coens* for short. The new organization added the degree of *Élu Coen*, or Chosen Priest, to the three degrees of Masonry. It was in the fourth degree that initiates learned the magical rituals of the order, cryptically called *La Chose* (The Thing).

Among the leading members of the order was Louis-Claude de Saint-Martin (1743–1803), an influential mystic. Upon Martinez de Pasqually's death in 1774, Willermoz and Saint-Martin became joint heads of the order; Saint-Martin eventually left the order to devote his time to the teachings of Jacob Boehme, and Willermoz merged the order into another Masonic body in 1784. The teachings of the Élus Coens survived and were passed on privately by initiates until the founding of the Martinist Order in 1884.

SEE ALSO: The First Masonic Grand Lodge (1717), The Martinist Order (1884)

Martinez de Pasqually, courtesy of Ordre Reaux Croix: The Three Branches of Martinism.

FRANZ ANTON MESMER COMES TO PARIS

THE HANDBILLS WENT UP ALL OVER PARIS, announcing a new and infallible method of curing disease through the use of a mysterious power called animal magnetism. In the days that followed, Parisian gossip overflowed with stories of strange devices, miraculous cures, and the physician from Vienna who was responsible for both. Franz Anton Mesmer had arrived.

Mesmer (1734–1815) was born and raised in a small town in southern Germany and studied medicine in Vienna, where he set up his practice. He became a Freemason and a little later was initiated into the Order of the Golden and Rosy Cross, the leading Rosicrucian society in Central Europe at that time. As he studied the occult lore of the Rosicrucians, Mesmer became convinced of the existence of a life-force that could be concentrated, dispersed, stored, and transmitted: a force he called animal magnetism. Never a modest man, Mesmer announced that animal magnetism was the only worthwhile method of healing, a claim that got him ostracized by most of the other physicians of Vienna. His move to Paris followed not long thereafter.

In Paris, he set up his equipment—water-filled wooden tubs studded with metal rods to discharge the animal magnetism—and began treating patients, putting them into healing trances. His clientele grew rapidly, and so did the hostility of the medical establishment, which called him a quack. A royal commission agreed with the physicians; the verdict was fiercely contested by his supporters and patients, but Mesmer had had enough of Paris and went to London and then elsewhere in Europe, seeking the acclaim he believed his discovery had earned.

After his death, practitioners of mesmerism quietly dropped the more occult elements and renamed their system "hypnotism," the name it still has today. Meanwhile, the more magical side of his teachings went back into the underground occult scene from which it originally came.

SEE ALSO: The Visions of Andrew Jackson Davis (1844), Birth of Spiritualism (1848)

1778

Engraving of a man hypnotizing a woman using the animal magnetism method, 1802, after Daniel Dodd.

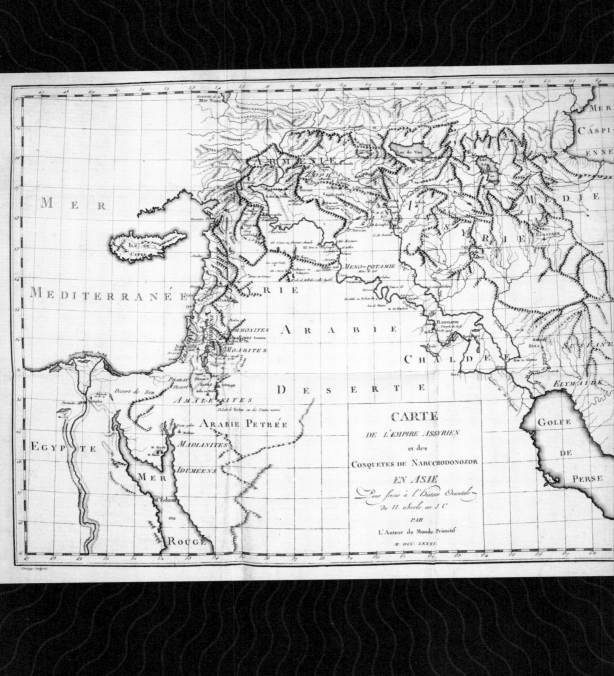

CARTE
DE L'EMPIRE ASSYRIEN
et des
CONQUETES DE NABUCHODONOZOR
EN ASIE
Pour servir à l'Histoire Occidentale
du VI. Siecle av. J.C.
PAR
L'Auteur du Monde Primitif
M. DCC. LXXXI.

MER MEDITERRANÉE

EGYPTE

MER ou ROUGE d'Edom

ILE DE CYPRE

SYRIE

ARABIE

DESERTE

ARABIE PETRÉE

AMALECITES

MADIANITES

IDUMEENS

MOABITES

AMMONITES

ARMENIE

ZOBA

MESO-POTAMIE

ASSYRIE

CHALDÉE

BABYLONE

MEDIE

MER CASPIENNE

SUSIANE

ELYMAIDE

GOLFE DE PERSE

TRACING THE TAROT TO EGYPT

EVERY ERA HAS SOMEPLACE IN THE PAST where it parks its dreams of a golden age, and in late eighteenth-century Europe, that place was Egypt. Little was known about the ancient civilization on the banks of the Nile, but that didn't keep writers of that time from filling in the gaps with their own enthusiastic imaginations. Antoine Court de Gébelin (1725–1784) was one of the most successful authors in that field, and in 1773 he issued the first of nine sprawling volumes of *Le monde primitif, analysé et comparé avec le monde moderne* (*The Primitive World Analyzed and Compared with the Modern World*), a lavish account of ancient Egypt as he imagined it.

The eighth volume appeared in 1781. In its pages, Court de Gébelin argued that the Tarot, which everyone in his time thought of as nothing more than an old-fashioned playing card deck, was the last surviving book of ancient Egyptian wisdom, miraculously preserved and handed down through the centuries. The word *Tarot* itself, which had

no meaning in any European language, he traced to ancient Egyptian: *tar*, he claimed, meant "road," and *rog* or *rosh* meant "royal." The Tarot was therefore the "royal road" to the wisdom of the ages.

In 1781, it bears remembering, neither Court de Gébelin nor any other living human being knew how to read a single word of ancient Egyptian, which wasn't deciphered until 1821. When scholars finally learned to read the hieroglyphs, it turned out that *tar*, *rog*, and *rosh* weren't Egyptian words at all; that the phrase *royal road* in ancient Egyptian is *w3t nsw* (pronounced something like "wa't nesoo"); and that nothing even remotely like the Tarot existed anywhere in ancient Egyptian art or literature. Despite this, the claim that the Tarot came from ancient Egypt became a standard feature of popular occult literature for the next two centuries.

SEE ALSO: Origin of the Tarot (1418), Etteilla Publicizes Tarot Divination (1783), The Rider-Waite Tarot Deck (1910)

A map of the Middle East, the frontispiece for the eighth volume of Court de Gébelin's *Le monde primitif, analysé et comparé avec le monde moderne* (*The Primitive World Analyzed and Compared with the Modern World*) (1781), in which he claimed the Tarot was a book of ancient Egyptian wisdom.

ETTEILLA PUBLICIZES
TAROT DIVINATION

JUST TWO YEARS AFTER ANTOINE COURT DE Gébelin claimed that the Tarot deck was a relic of ancient Egyptian wisdom, another writer published the first book on Tarot divination. His name was Jean-Baptiste Alliette (1738–1791), a working-class Parisian who happened to befriend an old man from Italy. The old man had learned to tell fortunes by using playing cards and taught his system to Alliette, who promptly turned his last name around and became Etteilla, fortune-teller extraordinaire.

In 1770 he published his first book, *Etteilla, ou manière de se récréer avec un jeu de cartes par M. * * ** (*Etteilla, or a Way of Entertaining Oneself with a Pack of Cards, by Mr. * * **), which taught readers how to read fortunes from an ordinary playing card deck. A book of astrological predictions followed in 1772 and then an expanded version of *Etteilla* in 1773.

The publication of Court de Gébelin's *Le monde primitif* seems to have struck Etteilla like a thunderbolt, and he acquired a deck of Tarot cards and began studying them at once. In 1783, the first of four volumes of Etteilla's masterwork, *Manière de se récréer avec le jeu de cartes nommées tarots* (*A Way of Entertaining Oneself with the Pack of Cards Called Tarots*), interpreted the Tarot in terms of Court de Gébelin's pseudo-Egyptian lore. His studies of the Tarot led him to take an interest in the entire occult tradition, and the years that followed saw him publish books on astrology, alchemy, and other occult sciences.

In 1788 he founded an organization, *Société des Interprètes du Livre de Thot* (Society of Interpreters of the Book of Thoth), to teach his methods of Tarot divination, and two years later he launched a more ambitious organization, *La Nouvelle École de Magie* (the New School of Magic). He died the next year, and not long afterward the school vanished in the turmoil of the French Revolution.

SEE ALSO: Origin of the Tarot (1418), Tracing the Tarot to Egypt (1781), The Rider-Waite Tarot Deck (1910)

Portrait of Etteilla from his book *Etteilla, ou manière de se récréer avec un jeu de cartes* (*Etteilla, or a Way of Entertaining Oneself with a Pack of Cards*).

ALESSANDRO CAGLIOSTRO DIES IN ROME

THEY FOUND HIM DEAD OF A STROKE IN HIS prison cell in the fortress of San Leo and buried him in an unmarked grave. All across Europe, word spread that the great Cagliostro (1743–1795) was dead.

His name was Giuseppe Balsamo during his boyhood in Palermo, and he spent some years as a novice monk before scandals forced him out of the cloister. When he was caught forging a title deed, he fled Palermo for Rome, where he met a beautiful teenager named Lorenza Feliciani, whose morals matched his own. The two of them soon were traveling from one city to another; he claimed to be Count Alessandro Cagliostro and sold magical elixirs, and she, as Countess Serafina Cagliostro, made herself available to a series of wealthy lovers—a line of work that gave her ample opportunities for blackmail and espionage.

In London in 1777, he was initiated into Freemasonry. Shortly afterward he claimed to have discovered an old manuscript revealing the rituals of Egyptian Freemasonry and promptly began offering initiation for a lavish fee. For the next eight years he was at the zenith of his career, a fabulously wealthy man of miracles.

When he and Serafina arrived in Paris in 1785, both were welcomed at the French royal court. The tangled politics of the time, though, ensnared Cagliostro; he was caught up in a major scandal and thrown into prison for a time, then banished from France. Then a Parisian hack journalist published an exposé proving that the great Count Cagliostro was none other than Giuseppi Balsamo, the small-time crook from Palermo.

That revelation destroyed Cagliostro's reputation and sent him fleeing across Europe back to Italy. There the Inquisition caught up with him. He was sentenced to life imprisonment and lingered for six years before death ended his astonishing career.

SEE ALSO: The First Masonic Grand Lodge (1717)

A colored line engraving of Alessandro Cagliostro, pseudonym of Giuseppe Balsamo.

IOLO MANUSCRIPTS.

A SELECTION OF

ANCIENT WELSH

𝔐𝔞𝔫𝔲𝔰𝔠𝔯𝔦𝔭𝔱𝔰,

IN PROSE AND VERSE, FROM THE COLLECTION MADE BY THE LATE
EDWARD WILLIAMS, Iolo Morganwg, FOR THE PURPOSE OF
FORMING A CONTINUATION OF THE MYFYRIAN
ARCHAIOLOGY; AND SUBSEQUENTLY
PROPOSED AS MATERIALS FOR
A NEW HISTORY OF
WALES:

WITH ENGLISH TRANSLATIONS AND NOTES,

BY HIS SON, THE LATE TALIESIN WILLIAMS, (AB IOLO,)

OF MERTHYR TYDFIL.

PUBLISHED FOR

The Welsh MSS. Society.

LLANDOVERY:

PRINTED AND PUBLISHED BY WILLIAM REES; SOLD ALSO BY
LONGMAN AND CO., D. WILLIAMS, AND H. HUGHES, LONDON;
MORGAN, & REES & SON, ABERGAVENNY.

MDCCCXLVIII.

DRUIDS CELEBRATE
THE AUTUMN EQUINOX

THE LEAVES WERE TURNING FALL COLORS on Primrose Hill on the north side of Regent's Park in London as a line of people filed out of a pub and walked through the streets toward the hilltop. Most were young, and all wore the colorful garments fashionable on the brink of Britain's Regency era; some had blue, green, or white ribbons tied around their right arms. Baffled passersby looked on as the group reached the hilltop and formed a circle. The leader of the group went to the center of the circle and called out: "Is there peace?" The people in the circle responded together, "Peace." For the first time in London since the banning of pagan religion, the celebration of the autumn equinox had begun.

The leader of the little group was a Welsh expatriate named Edward Williams (1747–1826), who went by the bardic name Iolo Morganwg. His background was impoverished and his early life a cascade of failures, but he claimed to have received from older bards in Wales a tradition of poetry and mystical wisdom dating back to the time of the ancient Druids. Brilliant, eccentric, and entirely willing to enhance whatever fragmentary traditions he might have been taught with his own inventions, Williams played a crucial role in transforming the vague popular interest in Druids and Celtic spirituality common at that time into a coherent movement—the Druid Revival.

All over Wales and in many other parts of Britain as well, there were people who wanted to learn the secrets of the Druids, and Williams was more than ready to teach them. In the years that followed that first equinox ceremony, supported by a growing circle of students and admirers, he passed on a free mix of tradition and invention to anyone who was willing to learn. By the time he died in 1826, Druidry had become a significant presence in the alternative culture of Britain and had spread to Europe and the United States as well.

SEE ALSO: Fall of Mona (57 CE), Ralph Blum's *The Book of Runes* (1983)

A selection of ancient Welsh manuscripts from the collection of Edward Williams, better known as Iolo Morganwg, published in 1848.

123

Talismans &
Magical Images
made from
The twenty eight Mansions
of
The Moon
&c. &c.

FRANCIS BARRETT'S *THE MAGUS*

D URING THE AGE OF REASON, OCCULTISM led a hole and corner existence in Europe. A few people continued to practice certain of the old occult sciences, but most of them worked in secret and concealed their activities from all but their closest associates. The era of persecution might have ended, but social pressures against occultism remained in place. Only now and then does some incident draw the veil aside far enough to allow today's researchers to glimpse something of the history of the occult in the Age of Reason.

One such glimpse was the publication of *The Magus, or Celestial Intelligencer*. It was written, or rather compiled, by Francis Barrett (b. c. 1770), an English occultist of whom almost nothing is known today. The book consisted mostly of lengthy quotations from Cornelius Agrippa's *Three Books of Occult Philosophy* filled out with bits of magical lore from other sources, accompanied by elegant illustrations and arranged as an introduction to magic for the English gentleman or lady of the Regency period. A note included with the text invited up to twelve persons who wished to take up the study of magic to contact the author.

At least one person is known to have taken Barrett up on his offer, one Dr. John Parkins of Grantham in Lincolnshire. A surviving letter from Barrett to his pupil provides detailed advice about the art of using a crystal to communicate with spirits and come into contact with spiritual realms. In the same letter, Barrett also offered Parkins the opportunity to be initiated into "the highest mysteries of the Rosycrucian discipline." What those disciplines were, where Barrett obtained them, and whether Parkins received the initiations that would give him access to them remain unknown.

SEE ALSO: Cornelius Agrippa's *Three Books of Occult Philosophy* (1533)

Colored diagram pasted inside the cover of *The Magus*, titled "Talismans and magical images made from the twenty-eight Mansions of the Moon, etc. etc." 1801.

JOHANN GEORG HOHMAN'S THE LONG LOST FRIEND

FROM 1682, WHEN IT WAS FOUNDED AS A British colony by the Quaker William Penn, Pennsylvania offered its citizens a right nearly unthinkable elsewhere in the Western world—the right of religious liberty—and that drew many Europeans who faced persecution for their beliefs to settle on Pennsylvanian soil. Many of them, like the Rosicrucians of the Chapter of Perfection described earlier in this book, came from Germany. They became known as the Pennsylvania Dutch (more properly *Deutsch*, "Germans"), and they brought with them a rich heritage of folk magic.

Johann Georg Hohman; his wife, Anna; and their son Philip were among those immigrants. Hohman found work as a printer and became one of the Pennsylvania Dutch community's most prolific music publishers. His press also issued religious works, some orthodox—for example, a Catholic catechism—and some rather less so—for example, the Gospel of Nicodemus, one of the gospels left out of the official version of the New Testament. Then there was *The Long Lost Friend*, which would be Hohman's lasting legacy.

The Long Lost Friend was a collection of household recipes. Treatments for common ailments accounted for a large proportion of the entries, as did such homely subjects as a recipe for gluten-free beer. A great deal of it, though, was Christian magic, including spells to banish fevers, catch thieves, ward off hostile enchantments, make bullets hit their mark, and much more.

To this day, *The Long Lost Friend* remains a primary sourcebook for folk magic among the Pennsylvania Dutch, rivaled in importance only by *The Fifth and Sixth Books of Moses*, a collection of Cabalistic spells brought over from Germany. Over the course of the nineteenth and twentieth centuries, it spread far beyond Pennsylvania to become a popular sourcebook for practitioners of hoodoo and many other kinds of American folk magic.

SEE ALSO: Rosicrucians Arrive in Pennsylvania (1694)

Pennsylvania Dutch Country has been home to various occult groups, from the early Rosicrucians to practitioners of Christian magic, such as Johann Georg Hohman.

THOMAS TAYLOR TRANSLATES ON THE MYSTERIES

THEY CALLED HIM THE PAGAN HIGH PRIEST of England, and he deserved the label. Born of working-class parents in London, Thomas Taylor (1758–1835) married his childhood sweetheart and supported himself with various day jobs, devoting his nights to study. He became one of the great classical scholars of his time, but reading Plato, Plotinus, and the Neoplatonists also converted him from a lukewarm Christian to a devout Greek pagan. Dreams of overturning Christianity and restoring pagan religion filled his thoughts, and with that goal in mind he began to translate the Greek classics into English. His first project was the *Hymns of Orpheus*, which saw print in 1787.

His translations and lectures brought him to the attention of wealthy patrons, who supported him to free up his time for more translations. One after another, the core documents of Neoplatonist philosophy appeared in English and became standard reading for poets, thinkers, and mystics. Meanwhile, Taylor practiced his religion openly, pouring libations of wine and sacrificing lambs to the Greek gods and goddesses as their worshippers had done two thousand years before. This brought down thundering denunciations from Christian authorities, and Taylor responded in kind, publicly describing Christianity as a "barbarous superstition" that someday surely would be replaced by resurgent paganism.

It was not until the 1820s, though, that Taylor took the risk of translating the core works of Neoplatonist magic and putting them in print. The first to appear was Iamblichus's *On the Mysteries*, the great manifesto of magical Neoplatonism that rallied the resistance to Christianity in the fourth century. Taylor's translation thus did for occult philosophy what William Lilly's *Christian Astrology* did for astrology: it placed the keys of an ancient occult tradition in the hands of anyone who could read.

SEE ALSO: Death of Plato (347 BCE), Plotinus Begins Teaching in Rome (244), Death of Iamblichus of Chalcis (330), William Lilly's *Christian Astrology* (1647)

Portrait of Thomas Taylor, c. 1812, by British painter Sir Thomas Lawrence (1769–1830).

THE VISIONS OF ANDREW JACKSON DAVIS

ANDREW JACKSON DAVIS (1826–1910) was a farm boy in Poughkeepsie, New York, the child of a poor and illiterate family. When he managed to become a shoemaker's apprentice, the local folks thought he had done about as well for himself as could be expected. In 1843, however, a traveling mesmerist came to town and put several local people into trance as part of a public demonstration. He didn't succeed in mesmerizing Davis, but when a local tailor tried again a few days later, the boy went easily into a trance and in that state was able to diagnose diseases and prescribe effective cures.

The next year, after developing a reputation as a seer and learning how to put himself into a trance, he had a tremendous vision in which he encountered the spirits of Galen, the Greek doctor in ancient Rome, and the Swedish mystic Emanuel Swedenborg. He awoke from that vision with the seed of a complex mystical philosophy in his mind. He immediately began teaching and lecturing and the next year began work on his first and most influential book, *The Principles of Nature*, which was published in 1847 and went through more than thirty editions in the three decades that followed.

The Principles of Nature and the many books that followed it, teaching his philosophy, established Davis as one of the leading lights in the burgeoning American alternative spirituality scene. His ideas were taken up by the Spiritualist movement, which burst on the scene in 1848, and spread from there to most of the occult traditions of the late nineteenth-century United States, helping to lay the foundations for the golden age of American occultism in the early twentieth century. His fusion of mystical philosophy with healing was at least as important as his influence on Spiritualism and played an influential role in bringing about the fusion of occult wisdom and alternative health care that later played so large a part in American occultism.

SEE ALSO: The Visions of Emanuel Swedenborg (1744), Franz Anton Mesmer Comes to Paris, (1778), Birth of Spiritualism (1848)

Portrait of Andrew Jackson Davis, born in upstate New York, who became known as the "Poughkeepsie Seer."

BIRTH OF SPIRITUALISM

THE RAPPING NOISES WERE SIMPLY AN annoyance at first, and the Fox family of Hydesville, New York, ignored them. Two of the girls, however, discovered that the noises would answer questions they asked. Gradually, they and neighbors who also interrogated the unseen noisemaker came to believe that they were communicating with the ghost of a murdered man whose corpse had been buried many years before in the cellar of the house.

Such tales have been common fodder for late-night storytelling since ancient times. Word of the Fox sisters and their conversations with the dead, though, spread rapidly through newspaper articles and word of mouth. Other people decided to try to talk to ghosts, and some claimed to get results. It was not until people familiar with Mesmerism found that a person in a trance could easily speak for the dead, however, that the religion of Spiritualism was born.

The new religion drew heavily on the writings of Emanuel Swedenborg and Andrew Jackson Davis for its theology and derived its practices from Franz Anton Mesmer's methods. In a classic Spiritualist séance, people hoping to speak with the dead sat in a darkened room with a medium who, after entering a trance, took on other personalities—first that of a "spirit control" and then those of dead relatives of the others who were present. Rapping noises often were heard, and stranger things sometimes were reported: tables levitating, spirit hands reaching out to touch attendees, messages written on slates in locked boxes, and more.

Some of these things actually may have happened. Others were certainly fraudulent. All of them helped feed the furor over Spiritualism. Over the years that followed, the new faith became a major presence in the religious life of most Western countries. In its wake, interest in more traditional forms of occultism also spread.

SEE ALSO: The Visions of Emanuel Swedenborg (1744), Franz Anton Mesmer Comes to Paris, (1778), The Visions of Andrew Jackson Davis (1844)

In a Spiritualist séance, people sit with mediums who attempt to contact the dead.

THE "VOODOO QUEEN"

NEW ORLEANS WAS ONE OF THE VERY FEW places in the slave-owning parts of the United States where a large community of free African Americans existed before the Civil War. Most of the members of that community were devout Christians, but some practiced religious and magical traditions inherited from their ancestors in Africa. After the Haitian Revolution broke out in 1791, refugees from Haiti brought the traditions of Vodoun to New Orleans to add to an already complex religious environment; from that heady mix came the traditions of New Orleans Voodoo.

Marie Laveau (1801–1881) was the acknowledged leader of the Voodoo community in New Orleans from around 1850 until she retired in 1869. She presided over ceremonies on the shores of Lake Pontchartrain on St. John's Eve, June 23, when hundreds of worshippers gathered around bonfires, danced to the beat of pounding drums, and took ritual baths in the lake. The rest of the year she could be found in her cottage on St. Ann Street, where she prepared and sold magical charms for a clientele that included wealthy white patrons as well as black people. When she died in 1881, every newspaper in New Orleans gave her a lengthy obituary.

New Orleans was the most important gateway through which African religion contributed a portion of its rich heritage to Western occultism, but it was far from the only one. All over the New World, African slaves clung tenaciously to their traditions and adapted them to fit the resources of their new homes. Although Vodoun and its New Orleans offshoot, Voodoo, survived in only a few places, a lively tradition of folk magic—known variously as hoodoo, conjure, and rootwork—blended more easily with the Protestant Christianity most African Americans practiced and became widespread. By 1900, practitioners of hoodoo could be found in most American cities.

SEE ALSO: The First Hoodoo Drugstore (1897)

A 1920 painting of Marie Laveau by Frank Schneider, based on an 1835 painting by George Catlin.

ÉLIPHAS LÉVI'S *DOCTRINE AND RITUAL OF HIGH MAGIC*

THE REAL NAME OF ÉLIPHAS LÉVI (1810–1875) was Alphonse Constant, but almost nobody remembers that anymore. Born in Paris, he was a shoemaker's son and spent his youth preparing for a career in the Catholic Church but realized he wasn't suited to a celibate life and went to work as a journalist and author instead. His first book, a political manifesto titled *La Bible de la liberté* (*The Bible of Liberty*), landed him in jail for a short time and gave him his first taste of fame, but the studies that would become his enduring legacy took him in other directions.

Pop culture in Constant's time wallowed in romantic notions borrowed from the Middle Ages, and scraps of the occult traditions of the past were among the things brought to light in that process. Whereas most of Constant's friends and associates treated those scraps as mere scenery, Constant sensed the presence of something much more important behind them: a way of understanding the cosmos that had lost none of its relevance with the passing years.

He plunged into an intensive study of the literature of magic and in 1854 published a slender book titled *Dogme de la haute magie* (*Doctrine of High Magic*). A second volume, *Rituel de la haute magie* (*Ritual of High Magic*), saw print the next year, and the two were published together shortly thereafter. Constant understood that prejudices against occultism remained solidly in place and so chose to publish them under the pen name of Éliphas Lévi.

The Doctrine and Ritual of High Magic presented the teachings of occultism in a form that made sense to Lévi's readers. Drawing on current ideas in philosophy and science, it built a bridge between the nineteenth century and the teachings of the occult, and a great many people crossed that bridge in the years that followed. Though there had been some stirrings of interest in magic before Lévi wrote, his book marks the beginning of the modern magical revival.

SEE ALSO: The Martinist Order (1884), The Hermetic Order of the Golden Dawn (1887)

An illustration by Éliphas Lévi of pagan deity Baphomet, published in *Dogme et rituel de la haute magie (Doctrine and Ritual of High Magic)*.

1855

JULES MICHELET'S *THE SORCERESS*

JULES MICHELET (1798–1874) WAS ONE OF the most influential historians of the nineteenth century, as popular among the French reading public as he was among professional historians. He had a talent for vivid description that brought the past to life for his readers, and he also loved to find unexpected angles from which to understand the past. When the great witchcraft persecutions of the fifteenth, sixteenth, and seventeenth centuries caught his attention, something remarkable was bound to come of it.

The times were propitious for such a reassessment. Europe in the 1850s was wracked by social unrest, and most governments banned political activism on the part of the poor; the poor responded by joining secret societies such as the Carbonari, which plotted assassination and revolution against the ruling classes. Michelet knew from his research that conflicts between rich and poor had been just as bitter in the late Middle Ages as they were in his time. What if, he suggested, the witchcraft that had been condemned so harshly by medieval lords and priests was a peasant secret society, a medieval equivalent of the Carbonari?

In his book *La sorcière* (*The Sorceress*), he used his talent for vivid portrayal of the past to imagine the rise, decadence, and destruction of witchcraft as a political secret society that was formed out of scraps of ancient pagan religion and rural folklore in opposition to an unjust social order and the church and state that defended it. The book became a best seller and influenced many other writers. Though later historical research disproved Michelet's theory, his conception of witchcraft ended up having a dramatic impact on the history of occultism, for it was to Michelet's vision, as reworked by later authors such as Charles Godfrey Leland and Margaret Murray, that modern Wicca can trace its historical origins.

SEE ALSO: Charles Godfrey Leland's *Aradia, or The Gospel of the Witches* (1899), Margaret Murray's *The Witch-Cult in Western Europe* (1921), Gerald Gardner's *Witchcraft Today* (1954), Wicca Goes Mainstream (1979)

Portrait of Jules Michelet by Thomas Couture (1815–1879), currently at the Carnavalet Museum, Paris, France.

EULIS!

THE HISTORY OF LOVE:

ITS WONDROUS MAGIC, CHEMISTRY, RULES, LAWS,
MODES, MOODS AND RATIONALE;

BEING THE

THIRD REVELATION OF SOUL AND SEX.

ALSO, REPLY TO

"WHY IS MAN IMMORTAL?"

THE SOLUTION OF THE DARWIN PROBLEM.

AN ENTIRELY NEW THEORY.

BY

Paschal Beverly Randolph, M.D.

THIRD EDITION.

TOLEDO, OHIO:
RANDOLPH Publishing Co.
1896.

THE BROTHERHOOD OF EULIS

PASCHAL BEVERLY RANDOLPH (1825–1875) was an American original. Born and raised in the slums of New York City, he was the illegitimate son of Flora Clark, a poor black woman, and William Beverly Randolph, a white man. His mother died when he was a child, and he led a precarious existence until his teen years, when he found a position as a cabin boy on a sailing ship.

In 1845, Randolph settled in upstate New York and took up Spiritualism as soon as it was born, becoming first a convert and then a medium. By 1853 he was holding regular séances, with a sideline as a "clairvoyant physician" specializing in sexual problems. He toured Europe three times, performing séances and meeting influential Spiritualists and occultists. Meanwhile he read Spiritualist and occult literature and began to develop his own occult philosophy.

During the Civil War years, he set aside his occult interests and helped recruit African American soldiers for the Union army. Thereafter, he began writing books on occult philosophy and practice and on human sexuality. In a period when most medical authorities insisted that women were incapable of orgasm, Randolph taught that regular orgasms were necessary for the physical health of both sexes and criticized men who ignored their partners' sexual needs.

On several occasions Randolph attempted to organize occult societies to teach his unique system of sexual occultism. He suffered from violent mood swings and an uncontrolled temper, though, and succeeded in wrecking each organization shortly after its founding. The largest and most successful of those orders was the Brotherhood of Eulis, founded in Tennessee in 1874. Like the others, it fell apart shortly after its founding, but it resumed work the next year after Randolph committed suicide. By way of the brotherhood, Randolph's teachings went on to influence many other occult traditions.

SEE ALSO: Birth of Spiritualism (1848)

Title page of the 1896 edition of *Eulis! The History of Love*, by Paschal Beverly Randolph.

THE THEOSOPHICAL SOCIETY

THE GROUP THAT GATHERED IN A RENTED hall in New York City that evening could have been any coterie of American occultists. In the wake of Spiritualism's golden age, such groups were common in every large American city. It's anyone's guess how many of those present that night noticed the stocky, dark-haired woman sitting among them or had the least hint that her appearance on the scene heralded a major transformation in occultism.

Her name was Helena Petrovna Blavatsky (1831–1891), and she claimed to be in contact with mysterious adepts from the East who promised to convey through her the secret teachings at the heart of occultism. Russian by birth, she ran away from an arranged marriage at seventeen. Her story was that she had traveled to Tibet to study at the feet of the masters; others told tales of her life as a circus performer, fraudulent Spiritualist medium, and adventuress. In 1873 she arrived in the United States and met Colonel Henry Steel

Olcott (1832–1907), an occultist and journalist with a talent for publicity. The two soon moved in together and drew up plans for the organization that held its first meeting that night in 1875: the Theosophical Society.

What set the new society apart from the many other occult groups in the Western world was its mission: to teach occultism to the public without vows of secrecy. Two massive books by Blavatsky—*Isis Unveiled* and *The Secret Doctrine*—helped spread the word, and over the decade that followed, branches of the Theosophical Society sprang up in every Western country. Though its history was full of scandal and controversy and Blavatsky was dogged throughout her life by accusations of fraud, the Theosophical Society became far and away the most influential occult organization of its age.

SEE ALSO: The Martinist Order (1884), Rudolf Steiner's Anthroposophical Society (1913), End of the Order of the Star in the East (1929)

Helena Blavatsky, Russian occultist and medium who co-founded the Theosophical Society.

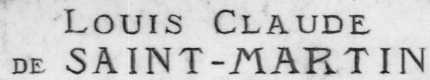

LOUIS CLAUDE
DE SAINT-MARTIN
"LE PHILOSOPHE INCONNU"

Est né dans cette MAISON, le 18 Janvier 1743
il est mort à AULNAY, près de SCEAUX,
le 13 Octobre 1803.

· · ·

LES AMIS de SAINT - MARTIN
1946

THE MARTINIST ORDER

D R. GÉRARD ENCAUSSE (1865–1916) WAS one of the leading lights of the French occult scene. A student of magical lore since his boyhood, he made his living as a physician but spent most of his free time in the Bibliothèque Nationale, the largest library in Paris, reading old books on magic and alchemy. He joined the Theosophical Society as soon as it arrived in France but soon tired of its increasing focus on Asiatic traditions, as he felt that his spiritual path called him to the occult teachings of the Western world. It was with this in mind that he borrowed a pen name from a list of spirits at the back of Éliphas Lévi's *Doctrine and Ritual of High Magic*—Papus, the physician—and it was as Papus that he began to write articles and, later, books on occultism.

At some point in the early 1880s, he was initiated into the magical tradition of the Élus Coens, which had been passed on quietly since the time of Martinez de Pasqually, and took up the study of the mystical writings of Martinez de Pasqually's student Louis-Claude de Saint-Martin as well. He and fellow occultist Pierre Augustin Chaboseau (1868–1946) decided to relaunch the ritual dimension of the tradition, which had been all but extinct since Saint-Martin's time, and in 1884 they founded the Martinist Order. Each of its three degrees of initiation came from a different source—the first, or Associate, degree from the Egyptian Masonry of Cagliostro; the second, or Initiate, degree from the Beneficent Knights of the Holy City of Jean-Baptise Willermoz; and the third, or *Superieur Inconnu* (Unknown Superior), from the system Encausse and Chaboseau had received from the heirs of Martinez de Pasqually.

By way of the Martinist Order, Martinism became a significant presence in the European occult scene in the early twentieth century, and by the end of the century it was to be found all over the Western world. It remains an influential presence in Western occult circles.

SEE ALSO: The Visions of Jacob Boehme (1610), The Élus Coens (1767), Éliphas Lévi's *Doctrine and Ritual of High Magic* (1855)

Plaque marking the birthplace of Louis-Claude de Saint-Martin in Amboise, France. His writings, and those of Martinez de Pasqually, form the foundations of the Martinist teachings.

THE HERMETIC ORDER OF
THE GOLDEN DAWN

O THIS DAY, NO ONE KNOWS WHERE THE manuscript came from. It was written in cipher and illustrated with crude drawings of magical symbols. Dr. William Wynn Westcott (1848–1925), a London Freemason and occultist, came by it somehow and brought it to his friend Samuel Mathers (1854–1918), another Freemason with occult interests. The cipher, they discovered, was in a Renaissance manual of secret writing by the wizard-abbot Johannes Trithemius; with that key, the two men decoded the manuscript and found that it outlined the rituals and secret teachings of a magical society called the Hermetic Order of the Golden Dawn.

Mathers expanded the outlines into working rituals, and Westcott used his contacts in the British occult and Masonic scene to attract members. By 1890 the Hermetic Order of the Golden Dawn was the most prestigious occult group in Britain, with a membership that included the Nobel Prize–winning poet William Butler Yeats. Members studied a curriculum of occult subjects, including Cabala, ceremonial magic, Tarot divination, astrology, and alchemy, compiled by Westcott, Mathers, and an inner circle of high-ranking members.

Unfortunately for the order, Mathers and Westcott fell out; Westcott quit, and Mathers turned out to be too unstable to manage it on his own. In a series of disastrous political crises between 1900 and 1903, the order tore itself into three fragments, each of which then faced further schisms and crises. By 1937 only a few scattered remnants of the original order survived. That year, though, the American occultist Israel Regardie (1907–1985)—who had been initiated into one of the surviving Golden Dawn temples in Britain—published *The Golden Dawn*, a collection of the order's papers. That proved to be the turning point; new, independent temples were founded, and today the Golden Dawn is far and away the most influential magical order in the Western world.

SEE ALSO: Aleister Crowley's *The Book of the Law* (1904), The Rider-Waite Tarot Deck (1910)

William Wynn Westcott, depicted here in the ceremonial garment of the Rosicrucians, co-founded the Hermetic Order of the Golden Dawn with his friend Samuel Mathers.

THE FIRST SALON DE LA ROSE+CROIX

THE ORCHESTRA PLAYED THE PRELUDE from Richard Wagner's final opera *Parsifal*. Incense wafted through the air, contending with the scent of hundreds of roses. On the walls, pictures by sixty-three artists attracted the admiring gaze of patrons, and outside the Galeries Durand-Ruel, the crowds were so thick that the Paris gendarmes had to close the street. The opening night of the first Salon de la Rose+Croix was off to a splendid start, and in the middle of everything, instantly recognizable by his long black beard and ornate robes, was Joséphin Péladan.

Péladan (1858–1918) grew up in Lyon and came to Paris as a young man, seeking a literary career. His scathing critiques of the mediocre paintings selected for the annual Paris salons won immediate attention and made him a leading figure in avant-garde circles. Like many young intellectuals at that time, he was fascinated by occultism and wrote a series of novels with occult themes. The first of them, *Le vice suprême* (*The Supreme Vice*),

was published in 1884 and became an instant bestseller.

A burgeoning literary career and an active life in the Paris occult scene weren't enough for Péladan, though. He wanted to give the Symbolists, a movement in the art world that focused on mystical themes, the exposure that the official Salon had denied them. That led him to conceive of a rival Salon, and the Salon de la Rose+Croix (Salon of the Rose+Cross) was the result.

The first Salon, in 1892, broke the grip of the official Salon on the Parisian art world, but it was the Impressionists and other avant-garde movements that broke through rather than Péladan's beloved Symbolists. Five more Salons de la Rose+Croix followed before Péladan admitted that his attempt to bring occultism back into painting had failed. He remained a prolific author, but he was nearly forgotten by his death in 1918.

SEE ALSO: The First Rosicrucian Manifesto (1614)

Portrait of Joséphin Péladan, 1892, by Alexandre Séon (1855–1917), from the Museum of Fine Arts of Lyon.

THE FIRST HOODOO DRUGSTORE

FROM ITS ORIGINS IN THE ERA OF SLAVERY, the African American magical tradition variously called hoodoo, conjure, and rootwork was practiced mostly by individuals who worked out of their own homes and gathered ingredients for charms in local forests and fields. After the end of slavery, though, black workers found jobs more easily in cities, and by 1900 most cities of any size had their own African American neighborhoods, with black-owned businesses and institutions. People living in cities still had needs that magic could address, but access to materials for charms was more difficult. In response, a commercial hoodoo industry emerged.

Among the core institutions of urban hoodoo were drugstores that sold candles, herbs, and other magical substances as well as ordinary medicines and personal care products. The first and for many decades the most famous of those stores was the Cracker Jack Drugstore on Rampart Street in New Orleans. Started as an ordinary drugstore by Dr. George Thomas, it quickly added hoodoo materials to its stock as Thomas learned what his clientele wanted to buy. By the 1920s the Cracker Jack had a reputation that extended across much of the United States, and hoodoo practitioners would travel long distances to buy raw materials there.

By then the Cracker Jack had plenty of competition; there were at least two more hoodoo drugstores in New Orleans, and most cities with a significant black population had one. Mail order houses supplied herbs, candles, oils, and powders to customers across the country despite postal regulations that defined their activities as fraudulent. Many hoodoo suppliers also carried books on Pennsylvania Dutch magic such as *The Long Lost Friend,* and as the twentieth century continued, classic works of Western occult literature also found their way onto their shelves, just as hoodoo traditions found their way into many other systems of occultism.

SEE ALSO: Johann Georg Hohman's *The Long Lost Friend* (1820)

Store selling occult items in the modern-day French Quarter of New Orleans.

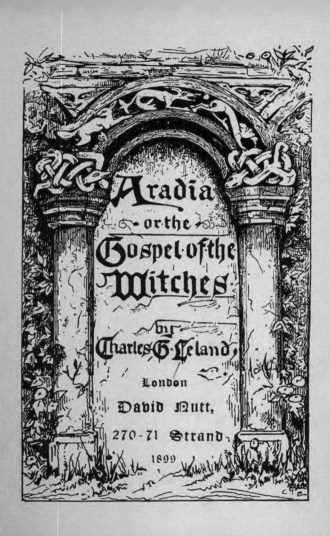

Aradia
·or·the·
Gospel·of·the
Witches

by
Charles·G·Leland,

London
David Nutt,
270-71 Strand,
1899

CHARLES GODFREY LELAND'S *ARADIA*, OR THE GOSPEL OF THE WITCHES

1899

HARLES GODFREY LELAND (1824–1903) led the kind of life more often found in romantic fiction than in the real world. Born to a wealthy Pennsylvania family, he learned folk magic from the Irish, Pennsylvania Dutch, and African American servants in his childhood home. He went to Paris as a young man, took part in the revolution of 1848 there, returned to the United States and fought on the Union side in the Civil War, and then worked as a prospector in the West before embarking on a career as an author and journalist.

Late in his life he moved to Florence, Italy, where he studied local folklore, seeking traces of ancient Roman and Etruscan traditions. In 1886, according to his later account, he first heard rumors of a secret book circulating among Italian witches. He succeeded in befriending one witch, to whom he gave the pseudonym Maddalena, and finally received from her a copy of the book, which he translated and published under the title *Aradia, or The Gospel of the Witches*.

According to the book, Aradia, the first witch, was the daughter of Diana, goddess of the moon, and her son and brother Lucifer. Because Diana pitied the poor and oppressed on earth, she sent down her daughter to teach them witchcraft to strike back at the church and state that oppressed them. All in all, it was exactly the kind of witchcraft that Jules Michelet had imagined back in 1862—and since Leland had read Michelet, that might not have been accidental.

To this day nobody knows if the book dates from sometime before 1886 or whether it was an invention of Maddalena or of Charles Godfrey Leland himself. Some scholars have suggested that Aradia might have been a historical person, an Italian peasant prophetess of the late Middle Ages around whom folk legends grew up. Whatever the source of *The Gospel of the Witches*, though, it went on to play a central role in the emergence of modern Wicca.

SEE ALSO: Jules Michelet's *The Sorceress* (1862), Margaret Murray's *The Witch-Cult in Western Europe* (1921), Gerald Gardner's *Witchcraft Today* (1954), Wicca Goes Mainstream (1979)

Title page of Charles Godfrey Leland's *Aradia, or The Gospel of the Witches*, published in 1899.

THE ELDER EDDA
COMMONLY CALLED
SÆMUND'S EDDA
EDITED AND
TRANSLATED BY
OLIVE BRAY.
PART I

GUIDO VON LIST'S VISION
OF THE RUNES

BORN IN A PROSPEROUS MERCHANT FAMILY in Vienna, Guido von List (1848–1919) broke with family tradition to become an author. At first he eked out a sparse living by writing nature articles for magazines, but he found a more lucrative theme with *Carnuntum*, his bestselling 1888 novel about Germanic tribesmen battling the legions of Rome. After several years of eye trouble, he underwent an operation in 1902 that required that his eyes remain bandaged for most of a year. During that year of darkness, he had a vision in which runes appeared to him and linked themselves with verses from the Elder Edda of the ancient Norse.

When he regained his sight, he was a changed man and threw himself into intensive research into the runes, ancient Norse and Germanic folklore, fairy tales, and occultism. His first book on the subject, *Das Geheimnis der Runen* (*The Secret of the Runes*), appeared in 1908 and found a ready audience all through Central European occult schools. He became convinced that many of the occult traditions of the Western world descended from ancient German sources and developed an extensive system of occultism that was based on his own interpretation of the runes.

With those teachings, though, von List blended popular notions about the superiority of the white race and of Germanic peoples in particular. From his work sprang a movement that called itself Ariosophy—"the wisdom of the Aryans"—that borrowed heavily from Theosophy but reworked it to support an agenda of pan-German racism. In the years before his death in 1919, von List proclaimed that a mighty leader, "the Strong One from Above," would soon arise and unite the Germanic peoples. He was, of course, quite correct; the year he died, an Austrian veteran named Adolf Hitler, who was strongly influenced by Ariosophy, began his political career.

SEE ALSO: Invention of the Runes (1st Century CE), Johannes Bureus Interprets the Runes (1611), The Thule Society (1917), Ralph Blum's *The Book of Runes* (1983)

Guido von List had a vision of runes linked with verses from the Elder Edda, a collection of anonymous poems of the ancient Norse. A title page from a 1908 edition is shown here.

ALEISTER CROWLEY'S
THE BOOK OF THE LAW

HIS FAMILY WAS SUFFOCATINGLY RESPECTable and his upbringing and education conventional, but Edward Alexander Crowley (1875–1947) was marked for an exceptional destiny. His mother helped things along by deciding that his teenage rebelliousness marked him as the Antichrist, an identity he enthusiastically adopted. Once he left home, he changed his first name to Aleister, wrote pornographic poetry, had sex with male and female partners, and got involved in occultism.

That led him to the Hermetic Order of the Golden Dawn, and he was initiated in 1898. The officers of the order in London found him too much to put up with and refused to initiate him into the Adeptus Minor grade, and so he went to Paris and talked Samuel Mathers into doing so—an action that helped spark the crisis in the order in 1900.

In 1903, he married and set out on a world tour with his bride. In Cairo, over three days in 1904, a disembodied voice dictated *The Book of the Law*, which praised passion and violence and gave him his enduring catchphrase: "Do what thou wilt shall be the whole of the law." Thereafter, as his marriage disintegrated and his literary career failed, Crowley became ever more convinced that he was what *The Book of the Law* proclaimed: the Great Beast 666, who would replace Christianity with the new religion of Thelema (the Greek word for "will").

From then on, Crowley's life was a chronicle of unbroken failure. He ran through the money he inherited from his family, his attempts to launch a magical order to spread the gospel of Thelema were blown apart by his erratic behavior, and a commune he founded in Italy got him expelled from that country. By the time he died in 1947, his followers could be counted on two hands and his estate was worth all of fourteen shillings. Not until the 1960s did his legacy become a force to contend with in the occult traditions of the West.

SEE ALSO: The Hermetic Order of the Golden Dawn (1887)

A 1921 portrait of occultist Aleister Crowley, writer, ceremonial magician, and self-proclaimed prophet.

THE RIDER-WAITE TAROT DECK

IN A CERTAIN SENSE, IT WAS A MATCH MADE IN heaven. Pamela "Pixie" Colman Smith (1878–1951) was a talented American artist with an interest in occultism; Arthur Edward Waite (1857–1939) was a lifelong student of the occult who needed an artist to create an innovative new Tarot deck. The two of them met by way of the Hermetic Order of the Golden Dawn, to which both belonged. In 1909, when the Golden Dawn had fallen apart and Waite was the head of one of the surviving fragments, he and Smith began work on the project, with Waite providing the symbolic content and Smith handling all the other aspects of the design.

In his research into the Tarot, Waite had discovered a fifteenth-century version—the Sola-Busca Tarot—in which the numbered cards of the four suits as well as the trumps had their own complex symbolic images. The new Tarot deck took the same approach. Waite drew on his extensive knowledge of magical symbolism and the Golden Dawn's Tarot teachings to provide each card with a memorable image; Smith painted the images in a crisp, instantly recognizable style that drew on her knowledge of the Symbolist movement in art. The deck was published by Rider & Co. in 1910 under the name of the Rider-Waite deck.

Waite remained an influential figure in the British occult scene until his death in 1939. Smith lived on until 1951, but her interest in occultism was already waning when she painted the deck. In 1911 she converted to Roman Catholicism, and she spent the rest of her life in relative poverty, eking out a living from book illustrations, sales of prints and paintings, and professional storytelling. It wasn't until the 1970s, when occultism became popular again across the Western world, that the Rider-Waite deck took its place as the most successful and influential Tarot deck of the twentieth century.

SEE ALSO: Origin of the Tarot (1418), Tracing the Tarot to Egypt (1781), Etteilla Publicizes Tarot Divination (1783), The Hermetic Order of the Golden Dawn (1887)

1910

The Sun and other cards from the Rider-Waite tarot deck, created by Pamela "Pixie" Colman Smith and Arthur Edward Waite in 1910.

CARL JUNG BREAKS WITH SIGMUND FREUD

IN THE EARLY YEARS OF THE TWENTIETH century, Sigmund Freud's (1856–1939) research into the unconscious mind kickstarted a revolution in psychology, drawing connections between suppressed sexual desires and mental illness that helped shatter what remained of Victorian morality. Among Freud's closest allies in the new psychoanalytic movement was the Swiss psychiatrist Carl Jung (1875–1961). In 1912, however, Jung broke with Freud, rejecting important elements of the older man's theories.

The central point under dispute was the role of sex in the unconscious mind. To Freud, everything below the surface of consciousness was dominated by sexuality and everything that came out of the unconscious—dreams, neurotic symptoms, slips of the tongue, and more—could be traced back to erotic desires that had been repressed in childhood. As Jung studied his own dreams, though, he found material that had nothing to do with sex but reflected themes he recognized from books he had read on the ancient Gnostics and the teachings of alchemy.

After his break with Freud, Jung pursued the connection between the unconscious and the occult and found example after example of ancient mystical and occult symbols in the dreams of people who had never encountered those symbols in waking life. He came to believe that below the repressed memories of individual life, there exists a collective unconscious full of archaic images that appear in myths, legends, and the traditions of occultism. By bringing those images into consciousness, it is possible to achieve individuation: a state of psychological balance and wholeness as far above ordinary sanity as neurotic conditions are below it.

All this was music to the ears of occultists, who recognized Jung as a kindred spirit. For most of the twentieth century, as a result, Jungian psychology became an important resource for occultists who wanted to make their ancient traditions understandable to a modern audience.

SEE ALSO: Dane Rudhyar's *The Astrology of Personality* (1936)

Group photo in front of Clark University, Worcester, Massachusetts, in 1909: Front row: Sigmund Freud, G. Stanley Hall, Carl Jung; Back row: Abraham A. Brill, Ernest Jones, Sándor Ferenczi.

RUDOLF STEINER'S ANTHROPOSOPHICAL SOCIETY

RUDOLF STEINER (1861–1925) WAS ONE OF the rising stars of European scholarship, the editor of a prestigious German literary magazine and the author of several books on philosophy, but his thoughts kept straying back to the Theosophical teachings he'd studied in college and the folk magic he'd learned from the old herbalist Felix Kogutski. He began attending meetings of the Theosophical Society's Berlin lodge, whose members were so impressed by his knowledge of occultism that they soon asked him to give lectures. His talks earned him a continentwide reputation; in 1912, he was elected president of the German section of the Theosophical Society.

Theosophy was in turmoil in those years as its leader, Annie Besant (1847–1933), took it in more and more erratic directions. In 1912, when Besant announced that an Indian boy named Jiddu Krishnamurti was the messiah, Steiner quit the society in disgust. Nearly all its German members walked out with him. Early the next year, most of them joined with him to found a new organization, the Anthroposophical Society.

Anthroposophy used Steiner's voluminous writings in place of *The Secret Doctrine* but kept Theosophy's mission of providing occult instruction to the public. In Steiner's hands, though, occultism—or, as he called it, spiritual science—took on a practical dimension it rarely had before. The biodynamic method of organic farming and gardening, an innovative method of education embodied in the Waldorf schools, and new approaches to art and architecture all flowed from Steiner's busy pen or took form in hundreds of lectures he delivered to audiences all over Europe. An international headquarters at Dornach in Switzerland that was founded in 1921 became the nerve center of the new movement. Although Steiner died in 1925, the Anthroposophical Society regrouped and remains an active presence in occultism.

SEE ALSO: The Theosophical Society (1875), End of the Order of the Star in the East (1929)

Portrait of Rudolf Steiner, c. 1891 or 1892, by Otto Fröhlich.

EVANGELINE ADAMS ACQUITTED OF FORTUNE-TELLING

1914

WHEN EVANGELINE ADAMS (1868–1932) visited New York City on that late winter day in 1899, she was already a well-known astrologer, and the owner of the hotel where she planned to stay eagerly provided her with his birth data. Adams calculated his birth chart and progressed it to that year, but what she saw disturbed her so much that she went to another hotel. The chart predicted disaster— a prediction that was fulfilled the next day when the hotel burned to the ground.

Word got out, and by 1905 Adams had so many clients in New York City that she moved there, renting a studio in Carnegie Hall and offering consultations. Her clientele soon included some of the richest and most influential people in New York, among them the legendary financier J. P. Morgan. When criticized for his interest in astrology, Morgan is reported to have said, "Millionaires don't use astrology. Billionaires do."

Under the laws of New York State, though, astrology still counted as fortune-telling and was against the law. In 1914, despite her wealthy and influential friends, Adams was brought up on charges of fortune-telling. To defend herself, she asked the judge to provide her with the birth data for a person he knew and she didn't and cast and interpreted that person's birth chart right there in court. The reading she gave was an accurate description of the personality of the judge's son. Impressed, the judge said that Adams had raised astrology to the level of an exact science and ruled that astrology no longer could be prosecuted as fortune-telling.

It took years for similar rulings to be handed down in other jurisdictions, but the climate of opinion had changed. By the middle years of the twentieth century, astrologers practiced their art undisturbed across most of the Western world.

SEE ALSO: The First Horoscopes (Late 5th Century BCE), John Dee Schedules a Royal Coronation (1559), Casting Spells for the Pope (1628), William Lilly's *Christian Astrology* (1647), Dane Rudhyar's *The Astrology of Personality* (1936)

Photograph of Evangeline Adams, taken in 1912 by Arnold Genthe (1869–1942).

THE THULE SOCIETY

THERE HAD BEEN OTHER SOCIETIES LIKE IT in Germany before and during World War I but none with so dramatic an impact on the politics of the time—or so infamous an offspring. It began as the Bavarian branch of an earlier German nationalist secret society, the Germanenorden (Order of Germans), but took a new name—the Thule-Gesellschaft, or Thule Society—to disguise its connection to the older group. Like the Germanenorden, it taught an explosive blend of Ariosophical racist occultism and extreme right-wing politics.

The Thule Society was little more than a year old when World War I ended and the German Empire collapsed. In the chaos that followed, a communist regime briefly seized power in Bavaria. The Thule Society threw its support to the conservative reaction, organizing a large militia unit and playing a central role in coordinating the counterrevolution that overthrew the Bavarian Soviet Republic in May 1919.

Far more important in the long run, though, was the Thule Society's decision to found a political group that would attract working-class members. At first, the Deutsche Arbeiterpartei (German Workers Party) made very little headway. One evening, though, a young Austrian veteran who had served with distinction in the Imperial German Army attended a meeting. By the end of the evening he had decided to join, and he went on to become the party's leader, changing its name to the National-sozialistische Deutsche Arbeiterpartei, or as it was later known, the Nazi Party. His name, of course, was Adolf Hitler.

All through the early 1920s, as the party became a mass movement and a major force in German politics, members of the Thule Society assisted Hitler in a variety of ways. By 1925, the society had quietly dissolved, leaving the field to its monstrous offspring.

SEE ALSO: Guido von List's Vision of the Runes (1902)

The Thule Society founded the Deutsche Arbeiterpartei (German Workers Party), whose most famous member, and eventual leader, was Adolf Hitler. Here Hitler speaks at a 1923 Nazi Party rally in Nuremberg, early in his rise to power.

CONTENTS

MARGARET MURRAY'S *THE WITCH-CULT IN WESTERN EUROPE*

IT'S HARD TO STUDY ANCIENT EGYPT WHEN you're stranded in Britain, and that was the predicament of Margaret Murray (1863–1963) when World War I broke out in 1914. She was an archaeologist and had planned to head to Egypt for a new season of excavation; the war made that impossible, and she decided instead to study the records of medieval witchcraft until the fighting ended.

In 1890, Sir James Frazer (1854–1941) had published *The Golden Bough*, which argued that many ancient myths and rituals came from an archaic fertility religion. Murray had read Frazer, and she became convinced that the persecutions of witches had destroyed a fertility religion exactly like the one Frazer described, which worshipped a horned god and met in thirteen-person covens on Candlemas (February 2), May Day, Lammas (August 1), and Halloween. She argued that when Europe became Christian during the Dark Ages, most of the rural poor kept their old religion until it was stamped out by three centuries of violent persecution.

By the time World War I ended in 1918, Murray had begun work on a book on the subject, *The Witch-Cult in Western Europe*, which saw print in 1921. Two more books followed: *The God of the Witches* in 1931 and *The Divine King in England* in 1954. By the time the last of those books was published, many historians accepted her theory.

It was only after her death in 1963 that a new generation of historians compared her work with the actual records and discovered that Murray had shamelessly manipulated the data, leaving out anything that contradicted her theory and treating details that appeared in one or two cases as though they were common. Scholars today agree that Murray's medieval fertility cult never existed. In the meantime, though, her theory finished the process of laying the groundwork for the rise of the new religion of Wicca.

SEE ALSO: Jules Michelet's *The Sorceress* (1862), Charles Godfrey Leland's *Aradia, or The Gospel of the Witches* (1899), Gerald Gardner's *Witchcraft Today* (1954), Wicca Goes Mainstream (1979)

The table of contents for Margaret Murray's *The Witch-Cult in Western Europe*, including topics such as animal sacrifice, magic words, and flying ointments.

ALFRED WATKINS
DISCOVERS THE LEYS

THE COUNTY OF HEREFORDSHIRE IN ENGLAND was green, unspoiled, and marked with the traces of past ages when Alfred Watkins (1855–1935) explored it in the 1920s. He worked for a local brewery and went from farm to farm to purchase barley and hops, traveling by horseback—the automobile was still a novelty in that part of England. One summer afternoon, while riding across the Bradwardine hills a few miles west of Hereford, he stopped on a high hilltop and noticed something startling. Before him, the relics of Britain's prehistory on the Herefordshire landscape—standing stones, burial mounds, holy wells, old roads of forgotten date, and the like—seemed to form straight lines. Tracing the lines on maps confirmed the impression: in some cases, dozens of ancient sites marked out straight lines across the landscape. Seeing that the lines on the map often passed through place names with the syllable *ley*, Watkins named them *leys*.

His first and most famous book on the subject, *The Old Straight Track*, proposed that the leys were the remnant of an ancient system of land navigation. In prehistoric times, when most of Britain was covered with trackless forest, traders and pilgrims needed to orient themselves as they journeyed, and Watkins argued that the leys served that purpose, providing sighting marks for travelers to follow. When his ideas were rejected by the archaeological establishment, Watkins organized a society, the Straight Track Postal Club, to carry out research on the leys.

Over time, Watkins and his fellow researchers began to wonder if what lay behind the ley system was considerably stranger than a system of navigation on land. Accounts of strange phenomena related to leys took up a large proportion of the club's correspondence in its latter years. The turmoil of World War II caused the club to fold, though, and it was not until the 1960s that other researchers picked up the loose ends of Watkins's research.

SEE ALSO: John Michell's *The View Over Atlantis* (1969)

The Malvern Hills, in the English counties of Worcestershire, Herefordshire, and northern Gloucestershire. Alfred Watkins believed a ley line passed along the hills' ridge.

HARRY HOUDINI BATTLES FAKE MEDIUMS

BY THE 1920S SPIRITUALISM HAD BECOME a familiar part of the religious scene all over the Western world. Spiritualist churches could be found in most cities, and there were also resort towns that catered to the Spiritualist trade, attracting hundreds of thousands of believers to summer events that combined recreation with séances. The most successful mediums claimed that the spirits that communicated through them could ring bells at a distance, write messages in chalk on sealed slates, and even manifest hands and other body parts made of a substance called ectoplasm. The difficulty was that many of those claims depended on outright fraud.

In 1924, a Smithsonian Institution committee called to investigate the famous medium Mina Crandon (1888–1941) invited Harry Houdini (1874–1926) to join them. Houdini's real name was Erik Weisz, and he was one of the most famous American stage magicians and escape artists, renowned for his ability to extract himself from handcuffs, straitjackets, and even more elaborate restraints. He accepted the invitation eagerly and went to Boston with the others to observe Crandon at work.

What he saw convinced Houdini that she was a deliberate faker, using a variety of stage magic tricks to produce the effects that made her clients think she was communicating with spirits and deflecting criticism with her personal charms—she liked to do séances in the nude and had had torrid affairs with several researchers who investigated her claims.

Unlike previous skeptics, Houdini wasn't content to put his objections into print. Instead, he went on the vaudeville circuit, doing performances in which he demonstrated exactly how fake mediums performed their supposed miracles. His campaign to expose fraudulent mediums was enormously successful, and along with increasingly harsh criticism in the media, it helped turn Spiritualism from a mass movement to a fringe phenomenon.

SEE ALSO: Birth of Spiritualism (1848)

On the stage of the New York Hippodrome, c. 1925, Houdini exposes techniques used by fraudulent mediums to an assemblage of New York clergymen.

THE "WARS OF THE ROSES"

THE UNITED STATES BETWEEN THE TWO world wars was a bubbling cauldron of occultism in which hundreds of different traditions, schools, orders, lodges, and other groups marketed their teachings to an eager public. For the most part, those organizations tolerated one another, but there were exceptions; the most colorful was the great contention between the two largest American Rosicrucian orders—the "Wars of the Roses."

The trouble began in 1925 when a New York businessman and occultist named Harvey Spencer Lewis (1883–1939) founded the Ancient Mystical Order Rosae Crucis (AMORC), which claimed to be the one and only heir of the original Rosicrucians. That brought an immediate challenge from R. Swinburne Clymer (1878–1966), the head of the Fraternitas Rosae Crucis (FRC), which already had claimed the same heritage. From that point until Lewis's death, the two orders hurled invective at each other, each insisting that the other was fraudulent.

Nor were AMORC and FRC alone in claiming the mantle of the Rosicrucians in the United States at that time. The Rosicrucian Fellowship, founded by Max Heindel (1865–1919) in 1907, and the Societas Rosicruciana in America (SRIA), also founded in 1907 by Sylvester Gould (1840–1909) and George Winslow Plummer (1876–1944), stayed out of the conflict but still fielded denunciations from the combatants from time to time. All in all, it was a confusing time to be a Rosicrucian.

Part of what made the conflict so heated was that all four organizations taught students by mail. This was the great age of the correspondence course, when millions of students all over the world signed up to receive lessons by mail in countless subjects—among them, occultism—and so all four Rosicrucian orders were competing for market share. The four orders still exist today and still offer their correspondence courses; fortunately, the old hostilities are long past.

SEE ALSO: The First Rosicrucian Manifesto (1614), Rosicrucians Arrive in Pennsylvania (1694)

Fountain at Egyptian museum in Rosicrucian Park, San Jose, California, the headquarters of the English Grand Lodge for the Americas of the Ancient Mystical Order Rosae Crucis (AMORC). Founder Harvey Spencer Lewis claimed that the order's roots began in ancient Egypt.

+ Omnia · ab · uno · et · in · unum · omnia +

THE FULCANELLI ENIGMA

PARIS BETWEEN THE TWO WORLD WARS was a hotbed of alchemy and other occult studies. In the bookstores and cafés where occultists gathered, rumors circulated about one who was not merely a student of alchemy but an adept who had made the Philosopher's Stone. No one knew where he had gained his knowledge; all they knew was his name: Fulcanelli.

Most of what was known about him came from the pages of two remarkable books. The more important was *Le mystère des cathédrales* (*The Mystery of the Cathedrals*), published in 1926; its sequel, *Les demeures philosophales* (*The Dwellings of the Philosophers*), appeared in 1930. Both books interpreted the architecture of certain medieval buildings as a guide to the alchemical Great Work, in the process displaying an immense knowledge of alchemical literature and a confident grasp of every detail of alchemical theory and practice.

Only in 1996 did the mystery finally unravel. In that year the French author and alchemist Geneviève Dubois showed that "Fulcanelli" was a composite figure. The original draft of *Le mystère des cathédrales* had been written by the famous occult scholar René Schwaller de Lubicz (1887–1961) and then expanded and revised without his knowledge by two other alchemists, Jean-Julien Champagne (1877–1932) and Pierre Dujols (1862–1926); *Les demeures philosophales* had been written entirely by those two men. The brilliant insights of the books had thus been the product of three of the best minds of the twentieth-century French alchemical revival.

A further enigma, however, remains. To the end of his life, Schwaller de Lubicz insisted that Jean-Julien Champagne had in fact made the Philosopher's Stone and transmuted base metal into gold. Did Champagne actually accomplish the Great Work? To this day, no one knows.

SEE ALSO: The Philosopher's Stone (1382)

Frontispiece of *Le mystère des cathédrales* (*The Mystery of the Cathedrals*), by "Fulcanelli" (1926); illustration by Jean-Julien Champagne.

The Secret Teachings of All Ages

Manly P. Hall

MANLY P. HALL'S *THE SECRET TEACHINGS OF ALL AGES*

ANLY PALMER HALL (1901–1990) WAS only eighteen years old when he caught the train in Sioux Falls, South Dakota. A few days later he arrived in Oceanside, California, where the Rosicrucian Fellowship had its headquarters. He soon moved on to Los Angeles, where he found work as a screenwriter and began giving lectures on occult philosophy. The screenwriting soon went by the wayside as his talks on occultism drew growing audiences. Despite his youth, he had an encyclopedic knowledge of occult teachings and a compelling stage presence. In 1923 he became the minister of the Church of the People, a metaphysical church in Los Angeles, and his Sunday sermons became must-see events for participants in the huge Los Angeles occult scene.

A year before, he had begun writing the book that would be his magnum opus. Funded by a bevy of wealthy supporters and lavishly illustrated by the artist Augustus Knapp, *The Secret Teachings of All Ages* was published in 1928 to immediate acclaim. In 1934, having established an international reputation as a major occult thinker, Hall founded the Philosophical Research Society (PRS) as a modern equivalent of the school of Pythagoras. He traveled to Europe and the Far East to research occult teachings and went on numerous lecture tours around the United States. Between those trips, he wrote more than two hundred other books on a galaxy of occult topics and gave weekly lectures at PRS headquarters until shortly before his death in 1990.

Some of his other books are widely considered classics of occult literature, but *The Secret Teachings of All Ages*—"the Big Book," as it's fondly called by Hall's students and fans—stands head and shoulders above the rest. The most important book of the early twentieth-century American occult revival, it remains influential, and many of the teachings and ideas it presented to the public remain in circulation even among people who have never opened its covers.

SEE ALSO: Pythagoras Comes to Crotona (6th Century BCE)

The cover of a 1978 edition of *The Secret Teachings of All Ages*, by Manly Palmer Hall, first published in 1928.

END OF THE ORDER OF
THE STAR IN THE EAST

IT HAD BEEN A LONG ROAD FOR JIDDU KRISH-namurti (1895–1986). The son of a servant at the Theosophical headquarters in Adyar, India, he had come to the attention of Annie Besant, who had become the leader of the Theosophical Society after Blavatsky's death. Besant convinced herself that Krishnamurti was the next World Teacher, a figure on a par with the Buddha and Jesus, and in 1911 founded an organization, the Order of the Star in the East, to promote that claim. Rudolf Steiner was not the only prominent Theosophist to quit the society over Besant's increasingly eccentric claims; two rival Theosophical organizations and Steiner's Anthroposophical Society had taken in some of these individuals and an assortment of other occult groups had drawn others, but the Order of the Star in the East flourished, attracting more than 100,000 members.

In 1929, Besant decided that it was time for her messiah to begin his public ministry, and a huge convocation of the order's membership was called at Ommen in the Netherlands. There, on August 3, Krishnamurti walked onto the open-air stage, looked out over the thousands of adoring followers before him, and proceeded over the minutes that followed to shatter Besant's dream forever. "Truth is a pathless land," he told his listeners, and no World Teacher or anyone else could lead them there. He denied that he was the World Teacher and finished the speech by dissolving the Order of the Star in the East. Krishnamurti went on to have a long career as a teacher of spiritual philosophy, but the Theosophical Society barely survived the debacle; like Spiritualism, it had invested too much of its credibility in failed claims, and it shrank to a small fraction of its earlier size and influence. Other occult organizations rose to prominence in its place.

SEE ALSO: The Theosophical Society (1875), Rudolf Steiner's Anthroposophical Society (1913)

Photograph of Jiddu Krishnamurti, whose elevation as a "World Teacher" caused a fissure in the Theosophical Society.

DION FORTUNE'S
THE MYSTICAL QABALAH

ORN AND RAISED IN A MIDDLE-CLASS English family whose only departure from utter respectability was an interest in Christian Science, Violet Firth (1890–1946) published two small books of conventionally romantic poems in her teen years. Two years at an agricultural college ended in 1913 with a nervous breakdown. Thereafter she studied psychology, qualifying as a lay Freudian therapist, and occultism, joining the Theosophical Society. In 1919 she found her most important occult teacher, Dr. Theodore Moriarty (1873–1923), who initiated her into a magical offshoot of Freemasonry. In the same year, she was initiated into one of the fragments of the Hermetic Order of the Golden Dawn, taking the magical name Deo Non Fortuna; later, she turned this into the pen name by which she is best known, Dion Fortune.

After Moriarty's death, Firth, who had been developing her own personal system of occult wisdom, decided that she was ready to begin teaching on her own. With five other occultists from Moriarty's circle she founded a magical order, the Fraternity of the Inner Light, with teachings that drew equally from Moriarty's work and that of the Golden Dawn. In 1928 her writing career began with an occult-themed novel, *The Demon Lover*.

Her most important book, though, was *The Mystical Qabalah*, published in 1935. Here she laid out in detail the entire philosophical and symbolic foundation of Golden Dawn magic. This and subsequent books became required reading in most occult schools in the second half of the twentieth century. Meanwhile, before her death in 1946, she trained an entire generation of British occultists whose writings and teachings helped fuel the occult boom that began to build in the 1970s. Her magical order, renamed the Society of the Inner Light, remains active, and so do several orders founded by her pupils.

SEE ALSO: The Hermetic Order of the Golden Dawn (1887)

Grave of Dion Fortune (born Violet Firth) at Glastonbury in Somerset, England.

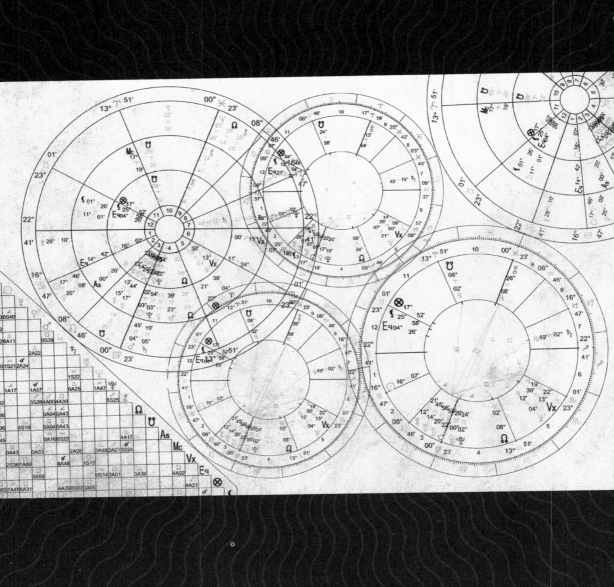

DANE RUDHYAR'S
THE ASTROLOGY OF PERSONALITY

ORN IN PARIS TO AN AFFLUENT FAMILY, Daniel Chennevière (1895–1985) was a child prodigy who graduated from college at age sixteen, published his first book two years later, and made a name for himself shortly thereafter as an avant-garde composer. Poor health kept him out of the trenches in World War I; instead, in 1916 he emigrated to the United States, where he wrote the musical scores for several early Hollywood movies and played an important role in the classical music scene. It was on his arrival in the United States that he changed his name to Dane Rudhyar.

In 1931 he moved to New Mexico, stopped composing music, and plunged into the study of occultism, with a special focus on astrology. The traditional approach to astrology, however, left him dissatisfied; he was less interested in foretelling the future than in using the stars to understand the personality, fusing astrological tradition with the insights of modern psychology and philosophy. By 1933 he had begun writing articles for astrological journals, exploring his new take on astrology, and in 1936 he published his masterwork, *The Astrology of Personality*, to immediate acclaim.

In the years that followed, Rudhyar's approach to astrology became the most influential current in the ongoing astrological revival, drawing on the same fascination with individual personality that made best sellers of books by Carl Jung and other psychologists. Rudhyar went on to write more than a dozen other books on astrology, and other astrologers influenced by his work took the same approach to astrology even further. In the process, natal astrology—the study of individual birth charts—became far more central to astrological practice than it had been, and many other branches of astrology were neglected. Three-quarters of a century would pass before the pendulum began to swing the other way.

SEE ALSO: The First Horoscopes (Late 5th Century BCE), William Lilly's *Christian Astrology* (1647)

Dane Rudhyar revolutionized astrology, turning its focus from predicting the future to focusing on individual psychology, popularizing the study of individual birth charts.

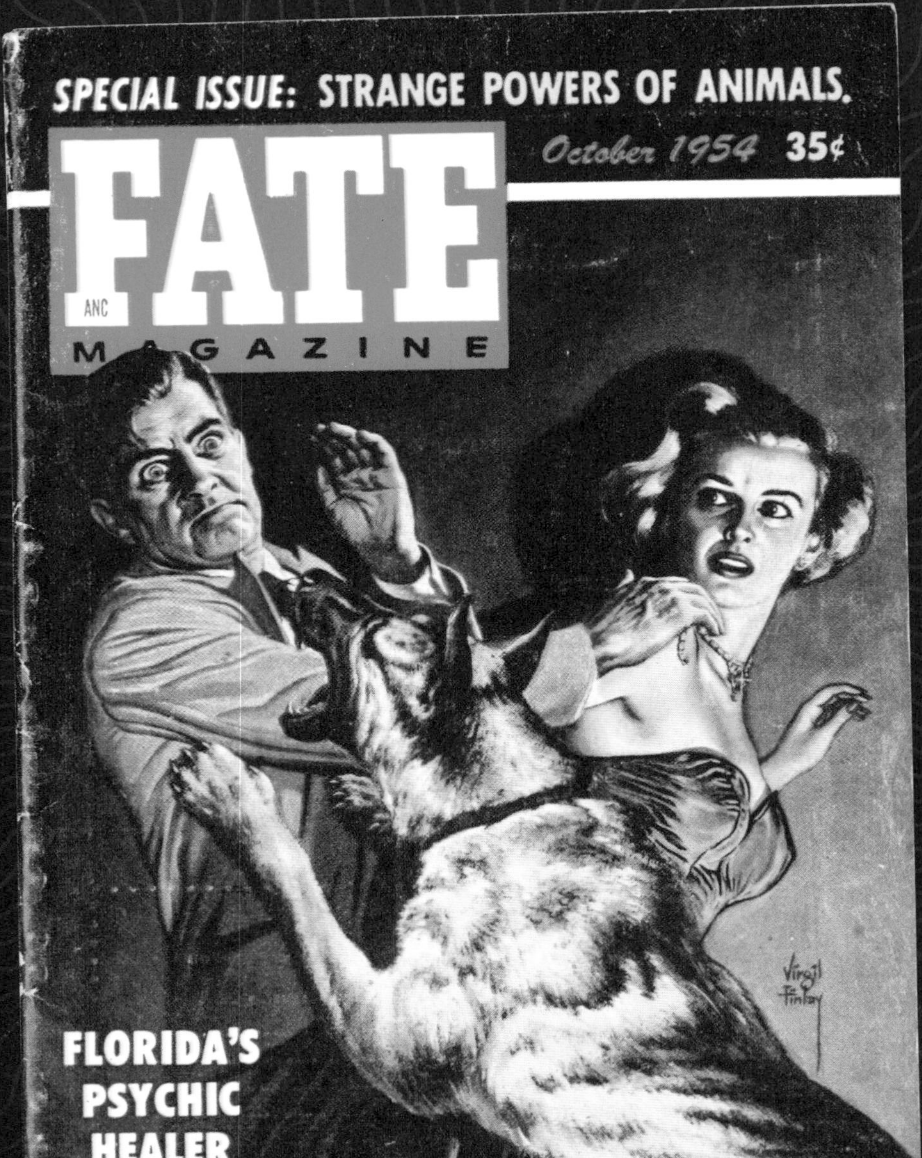

SPECIAL ISSUE: STRANGE POWERS OF ANIMALS.

FATE
ANC
MAGAZINE

October 1954   35¢

FLORIDA'S
PSYCHIC
HEALER

Virgil
Finlay

RAYMOND PALMER FOUNDS FATE MAGAZINE

PERMANENTLY DISABLED BY A CHILDHOOD accident, Raymond Palmer (1910–1977) found solace in science fiction fandom between the two world wars. In 1938 he made the jump from fan to professional when the Ziff Davis publishing chain hired him to edit the classic science fiction magazine *Amazing Stories*. Palmer's infallible sense for the lowest common denominator of literary taste promptly filled *Amazing Stories* with lurid and interchangeable tales of brawny space heroes, nubile maidens, and tentacled horrors; critics sneered, but sales boomed.

Like many science fiction fans in those days, Palmer was also interested in occultism and began including occult-themed stories and articles in the magazine to fill space when the supply of space operas ran short. Sales kept climbing. By 1945 *Amazing Stories* was dedicating more space to occultism than to standard science fiction, and the readers lapped it up. In 1948, though, his bosses in the Ziff Davis chain told him to drop the weird stuff and return the focus of *Amazing Stories* to spaceships, ray guns, and alien worlds.

Palmer responded by leaving the helm of *Amazing* and starting a new magazine of his own, *Fate*, dedicated to "true stories of the strange, the unusual, and the unknown." For the first time in modern history, alternative realities had a public forum; in among articles about flying saucer sightings, ghost stories, and tales of the sinister Deros, who supposedly inhabited a world of tunnels far underground, much traditional occult lore found its way into print. Meanwhile the classified ads in *Fate* became an important publicity venue for American occult schools.

Over the years to come, the mingling of occult teachings and other forms of rejected knowledge in the magazine's pages attracted a following. That following eventually became the New Age movement.

SEE ALSO: The End of the Thirteenth Baktun (2012)

Cover image from the October 1954 issue of *Fate* magazine, founded by Raymond Palmer after he left the helm of Ziff Davis's *Amazing Stories*.

Witchcraft Today

13

by GERALD B GARDNER

Introduction by Dr. Margaret Murray

GERALD GARDNER'S WITCHCRAFT TODAY

ERALD GARDNER (1884–1964) WAS PAST fifty when he returned to Britain in 1936 after a career in the colonial administration in Borneo and Malaysia and settled south of London in the New Forest. In the years that followed, he became a nudist, joined the Folklore Society, studied magic with Aleister Crowley in the Great Beast's final years, and made contacts elsewhere in the English occult scene. That much was agreed on by all sides in the controversy surrounding him.

The heart of the controversy was his claim that during those years he was initiated into a coven of witches that had existed in hiding in the New Forest since the Middle Ages. According to Gardner, members of the coven taught him their ancient religion, Wica (later renamed Wicca), a healthy, life-affirming pagan faith whose members practiced magic and divination. His books on the subject—*Witchcraft Today*, published in 1954, and *The Meaning of Witchcraft*, published in 1959—claimed to present as much of the traditions of Wicca as could be passed on to outsiders and found plenty of enthusiastic readers.

Critics pointed to the complete lack of evidence that Wicca existed before Gardner started writing about it and noted the far-more-straightforward connection between Gardner's claims and those of his friend and fellow Folklore Society member Margaret Murray. None of this had any impact on the popularity of Wicca. Over the decades that followed, Wiccan covens sprang up all over the English-speaking world and in some parts of Europe as well. Some of them were founded by people who studied with Gardner and his students; far more were launched by people who claimed, honestly or otherwise, to have been initiated into witchcraft through some other channel. All helped lay the foundations for the massive revival of occultism in the last quarter of the twentieth century.

SEE ALSO: Jules Michelet's *The Sorceress* (1862), Charles Godfrey Leland's *Aradia, or The Gospel of the Witches* (1899), Margaret Murray's *The Witch-Cult in Western Europe* (1921), Wicca Goes Mainstream (1979)

The 1954 cover of Gerald Gardner's *Witchcraft Today,* which helped popularize Wicca across the English-speaking world.

THE MODERN ALCHEMICAL REVIVAL

ALBERT REIDEL (1911–1984) WAS BORN IN Dresden, Germany, and grew up in the thriving German occult scene between the two world wars. Alchemy was a particular interest of his, and he met many German and French alchemists in those years, including the mysterious Fulcanelli. As the clouds of war gathered over Europe again, he immigrated to California, where he soon became involved in the Ancient Mystical Order Rosae Crucis (AMORC). During the war years, he attended classes in practical alchemy at the AMORC headquarters in San Jose.

He later moved to Salt Lake City, Utah, but continued his alchemical studies. In 1960 he founded a school named the Paracelsus Research Society (PRS) after the famous alchemist and healer, and he published *The Alchemist's Handbook*, the first widely available introduction to practical laboratory alchemy. Frater Albertus, as he preferred to call himself, made spagyrics—alchemical herbal medicine—central to the PRS curriculum and provided elementary instructions in several spagyric operations in his book. Both the school and the book were well timed; herbal medicine was beginning to catch a new wave of popularity in 1960, and interest in the occult was also on the upswing. The next two decades saw the emergence of a thriving alchemical subculture in the United States and elsewhere in the Western world.

By the early 1980s the Paracelsus Research Society had been renamed Paracelsus College, and Frater Albertus was preparing to found an actual college with its own campus of Gothic-style buildings, supported by the sale of spagyric medicines. His death in 1984 ended those hopes, and Paracelsus College closed not long afterward. By then, though, alchemy had resumed its traditional place among the major disciplines of the occult tradition.

SEE ALSO: Miriam the Alchemist (1st Century BCE), Zosimos of Panopolis (c. 300), Paracelsus Comes to Basel (1526), The Fulcanelli Enigma (1926)

Spagyrics, or alchemical herbal medicines, are made using alchemical processes involving distillation, fermentation, and extraction of minerals from plants.

JOHN MICHELL'S
THE VIEW OVER ATLANTIS

1969

B Y THE TIME THE 1960S ARRIVED, ALMOST nobody remembered Alfred Watkins or the long straight tracks he believed he had discovered running across the British countryside. The cultural turmoil of that decade, though, spurred new interest in many forgotten teachings, and two factors joined to transform leys from a footnote in archaeological history to a potent cultural icon.

The first of those factors was a young English author named John Michell (1933–2009) who had a taste for the mysterious and a solid knowledge of occultism. His first book, a contribution to the booming UFO literature of that time, has been almost entirely forgotten, but his second would not be. *The View Over Atlantis* revived Watkins's theories and combined them with a heady mix of occult teachings, sacred geometry, ancient myths and legends, and speculative history.

It would have remained just another piece of occult literature from a small publisher, however, except for the second factor: the mass market paperback boom. Starting in the 1950s, book publishers found that cheap pocket-size paperbacks could boost their sales to unprecedented levels. At the same time, more and more people felt disenchanted with scientific materialism and began to look for alternative viewpoints. Those two trends came together at the beginning of the 1970s to launch an explosive boom in occult-themed paperbacks.

The View Over Atlantis was among the pathbreaking titles in the occult paperback boom. It appeared in a mass market paperback edition in 1971, ran through two printings the month it was released, and kept selling steadily for years afterward. Michell went on to write many books on related subjects. Meanwhile, ley lines, sacred geometry, earth mysteries, and many other occult subjects found their way into popular culture, where they helped shape the burgeoning New Age movement.

SEE ALSO: Alfred Watkins Discovers the Leys (1922)

John Mitchell's *The View Over Atlantis* and other works centered on ancient myths and sacred spaces such as Glastonbury Tor, pictured here.

WICCA GOES MAINSTREAM

THE BOOKS WERE PUBLISHED ON THE SAME day—October 31, 1979—on opposite ends of the United States. In Boston, Beacon Press released Margot Adler's *Drawing Down the Moon*, a journalistic survey of the American neopagan counterculture; in San Francisco, Harper issued *The Spiral Dance*, an introduction to Wicca by a neo-pagan named Starhawk. Their simultaneous appearance marked the coming of age of Wicca as a pop culture phenomenon.

The Wicca that took center stage in those books and the thousands of others that followed them into print had changed dramatically since Gerald Gardner's day. What had been a secretive tradition passed on by personal initiation and concerned mostly with magic changed to a highly public religious movement that anyone could join by reading a few books, and it traded in much of its serious magical content for more familiar kinds of self-empowerment. Thus reshaped, it found an immediate audience throughout the English-speaking world.

For the first decade or so after Wicca found its feet as a pop culture phenomenon, the historical mythology created by Margaret Murray and Gerald Gardner—the claim that modern Wicca is "the Old Religion," directly descended from pagan cults of the Middle Ages that had nearly been exterminated in the Burning Times—was treated as historical fact by most of the neopagans. Gradually, however, the weight of historical evidence and negative publicity led influential Wiccans to abandon that claim. Similar motives led many of them to back away from occultism and begin a second reinvention of Wicca as a respectable religious denomination with paid clergy. In the meantime, though, the Wiccan phenomenon in pop culture made it possible for many other traditions to publicize themselves and attract a new generation of students, and many branches of occultism benefited.

SEE ALSO: Jules Michelet's *The Sorceress* (1862), Charles Godfrey Leland's *Aradia, or The Gospel of the Witches* (1899), Margaret Murray's *The Witch-Cult in Western Europe* (1921), Gerald Gardner's *Witchcraft Today* (1954)

Candles are used in many Wiccan rituals; pentagrams symbolize the five elements, including the spirit.

RALPH BLUM'S *THE BOOK OF RUNES*

I N THE WAKE OF GARDNER'S BOOKS ABOUT Wicca, the ancient pagan traditions of Europe became the focus of renewed interest across much of the Western world. Druid groups descended from Iolo Morganwg's reinvention of Celtic wisdom teachings went public, as did groups that hoped to reconstruct the religious and occult traditions of the Vikings. In the process, the magical and divinatory dimension of the runes, all but unnoticed since Johannes Bureus's time, was rediscovered and studied among small circles of students.

One of those students gave a set of runes to the cultural anthropologist Ralph Blum (b. 1932). In the wake of a personal crisis, Blum turned to the runes for guidance and found them a source of profound wisdom. His work with them resulted in a book and runestone set, which was published in 1983 as *The Book of Runes* and became a bestseller.

Purists criticized Blum because he changed the order of the runes, altered their traditional meanings, and added a blank runestone to the twenty-four runes of the elder futhark. Whatever merit there may be to those criticisms, Blum's work brought the runes to the attention of an international audience and created a market for other books on the runes. In the wake of *The Book of Runes*, furthermore, publishers began to bring out books about many other methods of divination. During the decades that followed, hundreds of previously unavailable divination systems and thousands of new Tarot decks became available to practitioners, and divination changed from an exotic activity practiced mostly by professionals to something that many people did on a regular basis. The growing interest in divination made it possible for other aspects of the occult heritage of the Western world to find students.

SEE ALSO: Invention of the Runes (1st Century CE), Johannes Bureus Interprets the Runes (1611), Guido von List's Vision of the Runes (1902)

A **1988 photograph of Ralph Blum**, taken by Jim Russell of the *Toronto Star*.

THE END OF THE THIRTEENTH BAKTUN

THE ANCIENT MAYAN CALENDAR GOT little attention except from specialists until the late 1970s, when rumors began to spread through New Age circles about December 21, 2012. That date marked the ending of the thirteenth baktun—a cycle of time 144,000 days long—and articles in New Age periodicals began to suggest that something big could be expected on that day. Toward the end of the decade, the drug guru Terence McKenna (1946–2000) settled on that date as the culmination of his "Timewave Zero" theory, which claimed that infinite novelty was breaking into our space-time continuum. It wasn't until José Argüelles (1939–2011) published his bestselling *The Mayan Factor* in 1987, though, that 2012 became a hot cultural property.

Over the years that followed, book after book rolled off the presses into the bookstores, insisting that the end of the Mayan calendar would bring utopia, apocalypse, or a blend of the two. Especially after 2008, when many New Agers in the United States found out that visualizing prosperity didn't keep them from losing their shirts in that year's real estate bust, 2012 became a magnet for the hopes and fears of millions.

Unfortunately for them, those hopes and fears were fastened to a phantom. There were no Mayan prophecies about the end of the thirteenth baktun; like most ancient peoples, the Mayans saw time as a cycle rather than a straight line ending in utopia or oblivion. The whole furor around 2012 was a product of the same kind of wishful thinking that had loaded messianic fantasies on Jiddu Krishnamurti and excused the frauds of fake mediums.

Thus the thirteenth baktun ended, and December 21, 2012, came and went without incident. The New Age movement suffered a body blow, though it is too soon to say whether that will prove fatal to the movement. Whatever the outcome, the occult traditions from which the New Age movement arose are still thriving throughout the Western world.

SEE ALSO: The *Prophecies* of Nostradamus (1555)

A representation of the Mayan calendar, consisting of cycles, or counts, with each named day appearing as a symbol or glyph.

Notes and References

Introduction

BCE stands for "Before the Common Era," and CE for "Common Era"; they are equivalents for the religious labels BC ("Before Christ") and AD (Anno Domini, "Year of the Lord" in Latin).

6th Century BCE: Pythagoras Comes to Crotona

Ferguson, Kitty, *The Music of Pythagoras* (New York: Walker Books, 2008).

Guthrie, Kenneth Sylvan, ed. and trans., *The Pythagorean Sourcebook and Library* (Grand Rapids, MI: Phanes, 1987).

5th Century BCE: Empedocles Invents the Four Elements

Kingsley, Peter, *Ancient Philosophy, Mystery, and Magic: Empedocles and Pythagorean Tradition* (New York: Oxford University Press, 1995).

Late 5th Century BCE: The First Horoscopes

Barton, Tamsyn, *Ancient Astrology* (London: Routledge, 1994).

Campion, Nicholas, *A History of Western Astrology*. Vol. 1: *The Ancient and Classical Worlds* (London: Bloomsbury, 2009).

347 BCE: Death of Plato

Plato, *Great Dialogues of Plato*, trans. W. H. D. Rouse (New York: Signet, 2015).

186 BCE: Rome Outlaws the Bacchic Mysteries

Bowden, Hugh, *Mystery Cults of the Ancient World* (Princeton, NJ: Princeton University Press, 2010).

Livy, *Rome and the Mediterranean: The History of Rome*, books 31–45, trans. Henry Bettenson (New York: Penguin, 1976).

1st Century BCE: Miriam the Alchemist

Lindsay, Jack, *The Origins of Alchemy in Graeco-Roman Egypt* (New York: Barnes & Noble, 1970).

Patai, Raphael, *The Jewish Alchemists* (Princeton, NJ: Princeton University Press, 1994).

33 CE: Death of Jesus

Fideler, David R., *Jesus Christ, Sun of God* (Wheaton, IL.: Quest, 1993).

Smith, Morton, *Jesus the Magician* (San Francisco: Harper & Row, 1978).

57 CE: Fall of Mona

Ellis, Peter Beresford, *The Druids* (London: Constable, 1994).

c. 1st Century CE: Invention of the Runes

Flowers, Stephen, *Runes and Magic* (Berne, Switzerland: Peter Lange, 1986).

1st Century CE: Apollonius of Tyana

Mead, G. R. S., *Apollonius of Tyana* (New Hyde Park, NY: University Books, 1966).

c. 120: Basilides of Alexandria

Culianu, Ioan, *The Tree of Gnosis* (San Francisco: HarperCollins, 1992).

Layton, Bentley, *The Gnostic Scriptures* (Garden City, NY: Doubleday, 1987).

2nd century: Magic on Trial

Apuleius, Lucius, *The Apology* (his defense against charges of magic, out of print but available on many websites).

———*The Golden Ass*, trans. E. J. Penney (New York: Penguin, 1999).

155: Valentinus Loses a Papal Election

Layton, Bentley, *The Gnostic Scriptures* (Garden City, NY: Doubleday, 1987).

Pagels, Elaine, *The Origin of Satan* (New York: Vintage, 1996).

3rd Century: *The Corpus Hermeticum*

Fowden, Garth, *The Egyptian Hermes* (Princeton, NJ: Princeton University Press, 1986).

244: Plotinus Begins Teaching in Rome

Plotinus, *The Enneads*, trans. Stephen MacKenna (Burdett, NY: Larson, 1992).

Wallis, R. T., *Neoplatonism* (New York: Scribner's, 1972).

c. 300: Zosimos of Panopolis

Lindsay, Jack, *The Origins of Alchemy in Graeco-Roman Egypt* (New York: Barnes & Noble, 1970).

330: Death of Iamblichus of Chalcis
Shaw, Gregory, *Theurgy and the Soul: The Neoplatonism of Iamblichus* (University Park: Pennsylvania State University Press, 1995).

363: Last Pagan Emperor of Rome
Julian the Apostate, *Emperor and Author: The Writings of Julian the Apostate* (Swansea, UK: Classical Press of Wales, 2012).
Murdoch, Adrian, *The Last Pagan: Julian the Apostate and the Death of the Ancient World* (Rutland, VT: Inner Traditions, 2008).

396: End of the Eleusinian Mysteries
Kerenyi, Carl, *Eleusis* (New York: Bollingen Foundation, 1967).
Mylonas, George E., *Eleusis and the Eleusinian Mysteries* (Princeton, NJ: Princeton University Press, 1961).

538: The Edicts of Justinian
Chuvin, Pierre, *A Chronicle of the Last Pagans*, trans. B. A. Archer (Cambridge, MA: Harvard University Press, 1989).

573: Merlin and the Battle of Arderydd
Tolstoy, Nicholas, *The Quest for Merlin* (Boston: Little, Brown, 1985).

c. 800: Jabir ibn Hayyan
Haq, Syed Nomanul, *Names, Natures and Things: The Alchemist Jabir ibn Hayyan and His "Kitab al Ahjar" (Book of Stones)* (Boston: Kluwer, 1994).

9th Century: Canon *Episcopi*
Ginzburg, Carlo, *Ecstasies: Deciphering the Witches' Sabbath* (New York: Pantheon, 1991).

1118: Founding of the Knights Templar
Barber, Malcolm, *The New Knighthood: A History of the Order of the Temple* (New York: Cambridge University Press, 1994).
Upton-Ward, J. M., trans., *The Rule of the Templars: The French Text of the Rule of the Order of the Knights Templar* (Woodbridge, Suffolk: Boydell, 1992).

1208: The Albigensian Crusade
Barber, Malcolm, *The Cathars* (Harlow, UK: Longman, 2000).
Guirdham, Arthur, *The Great Heresy* (Jersey, UK: Neville Spearman, 1977).

c. 1230: Origins of the Cabala
Scholem, Gershom, *The Kabbalah* (New York: Quadrangle, 1974).
——*Origins of the Kabbalah* (Princeton, NJ: Princeton University Press, 1987).

1256: Translation of *Picatrix*
Greer, John Michael, and Christopher Warnock, trans., *The Picatrix* (Iowa City, IA: Adocentyn Press, 2011).

1271: Fall of Harran
Green, Tamara M., *City of the Moon God: Religious Traditions of Harran* (Leiden, Netherlands: Brill, 1992).

1279: Abraham Abulafia Goes to Saronno
Idel, Moshe, *The Mystical Experience in Abraham Abulafia* (Albany: State University of New York Press, 1988).

1307: Arrest of the Knights Templar
Barber, Malcolm, *The Trial of the Templars* (New York: Cambridge University Press, 1978).
Partner, Peter, *The Murdered Magicians: The Templars and Their Myth* (Oxford, UK: Oxford University Press, 1982).

1327: Cecco d'Ascoli Burned at the Stake
Thorndyke, Lynn, *The History of Magic and Experimental Science*, vol. 2 (New York: Macmillan, 1934).

1382: The Philosopher's Stone
Flamel, Nicholas, *Nicholas Flamel: His Exposition of the Hieroglyphical Figures* (New York: Garland Press, 1994).

1418: Origin of the Tarot
Dummett, Michael, *The Visconti-Sforza Tarot Cards* (New York: George Braziller, 1986).

1428: The Great Valais Witch Trials Begin
Ginzburg, Carlo, *Ecstasies: Deciphering the Witch's Sabbath* (New York: Pantheon, 1991).
Kieckhefer, Richard, *European Witch Trials* (Berkeley: University of California Press, 1976).

1464: Translation of the *Corpus Hermeticum*
Yates, Frances, *Giordano Bruno and the Hermetic Tradition* (Chicago: University of Chicago Press, 1964).

1486: The *Malleus Maleficarum*
Cohn, Norman, *Europe's Inner Demons* (New York: Basic Books, 1975).
Kramer, Heinrich, and Jacob Sprenger, *Malleus Maleficarum*, trans. Montague Summers (New York: Dover, 1971).

1494: Johannes Reuchlin's *On the Miraculous Word*
Blau, Joseph Leon, *The Christian Interpretation of the Cabala in the Renaissance* (New York: Columbia University Press, 1944).
Reuchlin, Johann, *On the Art of the Cabala*, trans. Martin Goodman and Sarah Goodman (Lincoln, NB: Bison, 1993).

1526: Paracelsus Comes to Basel
Grell, Ole Peter, ed., *Paracelsus: The Man and His Reputation* (Leiden, Netherlands: Brill, 1998).
Paracelsus, *Essential Readings*, ed. Nicholas Goodrick-Clarke (Wellingborough, UK: Crucible, 1990).

1533: Cornelius Agrippa's *Three Books of Occult Philosophy*
Agrippa, Henry Cornelius, *Three Books of Occult Philosophy*, ed. Donald Tyson (St. Paul, MN: Llewellyn, 1993).

1555: The *Prophecies* of Nostradamus
Cheetham, Erika, ed., *The Complete Prophecies of Nostradamus* (New York: Berkley Books, 1981).
Gerson, Stéphane, *Nostradamus: How an Obscure Renaissance Astrologer Became the Modern Prophet of Doom* (New York: St. Martin's Press, 2012).

1559: John Dee Schedules a Royal Coronation
Suster, Gerald, ed., *John Dee: Essential Readings* (San Francisco: North Atlantic Books, 2003).
Wooley, Benjamin, *The Queen's Conjurer* (New York: Henry Holt, 2001).

1570: Isaac Luria Arrives in Safed
Dunn, James David, *Window of the Soul: The Kabbalah of Rabbi Isaac Luria* (York Beach, ME: Weiser Books, 2008).
Fine, Lawrence, *Physician of the Soul, Healer of the Cosmos* (Stanford, CA: Stanford University Press, 2003).

1575: The *Benandanti*
Ginzburg, Carlo, *The Night Battles* (New York: Penguin, 1985).

1587: The Legend of Faust
Baron, Frank, *Doctor Faustus: From History to Legend* (Munich: Wilhelm Fink, 1978).
Butler, E. M., *The Fortunes of Faust* (Cambridge, UK: Cambridge University Press, 1952).

1600: Giordano Bruno Burned at the Stake
Rowland, Ingrid D., *Giordano Bruno: Philosopher/Heretic* (Chicago: University of Chicago Press, 2009).
Yates, Frances, *Giordano Bruno and the Hermetic Tradition* (Chicago: University of Chicago Press, 1964).

1610: The Visions of Jacob Boehme
Boehme, Jakob, *Essential Readings*, ed. Robin Waterfield (Wellingborough, UK: Aquarian, 1989).

1611: Johannes Bureus Interprets the Runes
Åkerman, Susanna, *Rose Cross over the Baltic* (Leiden, Netherlands: Brill, 1998).
Flowers, Stephen, *Johannes Bureus and Adalruna* (Austin, TX: Runa-Raven, 1998).

1614: The First Rosicrucian Manifesto
Allen, Paul A., ed., *A Christian Rosenkreutz Anthology* (Blauvelt, NY: Rudolf Steiner Publications, 1968).
Yates, Frances, *The Rosicrucian Enlightenment* (London: Routledge & Kegan Paul, 1972).

1628: Casting Spells for the Pope
Campanella, Tommaso, *The City of the Sun*, trans. Daniel J. Donno (Berkeley: University of California Press, 1981).
Headley, John M., *Tommaso Campanella and the Transformation of the World* (Princeton, NJ: Princeton University Press, 1997).

1630: Gerard Thibault's *Academy of the Sword*
Thibault, Gerard, *Academy of the Sword*, trans. John Michael Greer (London: Aeon Books, 2017).

1647: William Lilly's *Christian Astrology*
Geneva, Ann, *Astrology and the Seventeenth-Century Mind* (Manchester, UK: Manchester University Press, 1995).

1694: Rosicrucians Arrive in Pennsylvania
Churton, Tobias, *The Invisible History of the Rosicrucians* (Rutland, VT: Inner Traditions, 2009).
McIntosh, Christopher, *The Rosicrucians: The History and Mythology of an Occult Order* (Wellingborough, UK: Aquarian, 1987).

1717: The First Masonic Grand Lodge
Stevenson, David, *The Origins of Freemasonry* (Cambridge: Cambridge University Press, 1988).

1736: Passage of the Witchcraft Act
Davies, Owen, *Witchcraft, Magic and Culture 1736–1951* (Manchester, UK: Manchester University Press, 1999).

1744: The Visions of Emanuel Swedenborg
Trobridge, George, *Swedenborg: Life and Teaching* (New York: Swedenborg Foundation, 1992).

1746: Founding of the Hellfire Club
Towers, Eric, *Dashwood—The Man and the Myth* (Wellingborough, UK: Crucible, 1987).

1767: The Élus Coens
Waite, Arthur Edward, *The Unknown Philosopher* (London: Steiner Books, 1970).

1778: Franz Anton Mesmer Comes to Paris
Buranelli, Vincent, *The Wizard from Vienna* (New York: Coward McCann, 1975).
Mesmer, Franz Anton, *Mesmerism* (London: Macdonald, 1948).

1781: Tracing the Tarot to Egypt
Decker, Ronald, Thierry DePaulis, and Michael Dummett, *A Wicked Pack of Cards: Origins of the Occult Tarot* (New York: St. Martin's, 1996).

1783: Etteilla Publicizes Tarot Divination
Decker, Ronald, Thierry DePaulis, and Michael Dummett, *A Wicked Pack of Cards: Origins of the Occult Tarot* (New York: St. Martin's, 1996).

1795: Alessandro Cagliostro Dies in Rome
Faulks, Philippa, and Robert L. D. Cooper, *The Masonic Magician* (London: Watkins, 2008).
McCalman, Iain, *The Last Alchemist* (New York: Harper Perennial, 2004).

1798: Druids Celebrate the Autumn Equinox
Jenkins, Geraint H., *Facts, Fantasy, and Fiction: The Historical Vision of Iolo Morganwg* (Aberystwyth, Wales: Canolfan Uwchefrydiau Cymreig a Cheltaidd Prifysgol Cymry, 1997).

1801: Francis Barrett's *The Magus*
Barrett, Francis, *The Magus* (York Beach, ME: Weiser, 2000).

1820: Johann Georg Hohman's *The Long Lost Friend*
Hohman, John George, *The Long Lost Friend*, ed. Daniel Harms (Woodbury, MN: Llewellyn, 2012).

1821: Thomas Taylor Translates *On the Mysteries*
Taylor, Thomas, *Thomas Taylor the Platonist*, ed. Kathleen Raine and George Mills Harper (Princeton, NJ: Princeton University Press, 1969).

1844: The Visions of Andrew Jackson Davis
Davis, Andrew Jackson, *The Magic Staff: An Autobiography of Andrew Jackson Davis* (Mokelumne Hill, CA: Health Research, 1970).

1848: Birth of Spiritualism
Leonard, Maurice, *People from the Other Side* (Stroud, UK; History Press, 2008).
Weisberg, Barbara: *Talking to the Dead: The Story of the Fox Sisters* (New York: HarperOne, 2005).

c. 1850: The "Voodoo Queen"
Long, Carolyn Morrow, *Spiritual Merchants: Religion, Magic, and Commerce* (Knoxville: University of Tennessee Press, 2001).

1855: Éliphas Lévi's *Doctrine and Ritual of High Magic*
Lévi, Éliphas, *Doctrine and Ritual of High Magic*, trans. John Michael Greer and Mark Anthony Mikituk (New York: Tarcher/ Penguin, 2017).
Williams, Thomas A., *Eliphas Levi, Master of Occultism* (Tuscaloosa, AL: University of Alabama Press, 1975).

1862: Jules Michelet's *The Sorceress*
Michelet, Jules, *Satanism and Witchcraft*, trans. A. R. Allinson (London: Tandem Books, 1969).

1874: The Brotherhood of Eulis
Deveny, John, *Paschal Beverly Randolph* (Albany: State University of New York Press, 1997).

1875: The Theosophical Society
Cranston, Sylvia, *H. P. B.* (New York: TarcherPerigee, 1993).
Washington, Peter, *Madam Blavatsky's Baboon* (New York: Schocken Books, 1993).

1884: The Martinist Order
Churton, Tobias, *Occult Paris* (Rutland, VT: Inner Traditions, 2016).

1887: The Hermetic Order of the Golden Dawn
Howe, Ellic, *The Magicians of the Golden Dawn* (London: Routledge & Kegan Paul, 1972).
Regardie, Israel, *The Golden Dawn*, revised seventh edition (Woodbury, MN: Llewelyn Worldwide, 2016).

1892: The First Salon de la Rose+Croix
Pincus-Witten, Robert, *Occult Symbolism in France: Joséphin Péladan and the Salons de la Rose-Croix* (New York: Garland, 1976).

1897: The First Hoodoo Drugstore
Long, Carolyn Morrow, *Spiritual Merchants: Religion, Magic, and Commerce* (Knoxville: University of Tennessee Press, 2001).

1899: Charles Godfrey Leland's *Aradia, or The Gospel of the Witches*
Leland, Charles Godfrey, *Aradia, or the Gospel of the Witches* (New York: Samuel Weiser, 1974).

1902: Guido von List's Vision of the Runes
Goodrick-Clarke, Nicholas, *The Occult Roots of Nazism* (New York: New York University Press, 1992).
von List, Guido, *The Secret of the Runes* (Rutland, VT: Inner Traditions, 1988).

1904: Aleister Crowley's *The Book of the Law*
Crowley, Aleister, *The Book of the Law* (York Beach, ME: Weiser Books, 1987).
Kaczynski, Richard, *Perdurabo* (San Francisco: North Atlantic Books, 2010).

1910: The Rider-Waite Tarot Deck
Decker, Ronald, and Michael Dummett, *A History of the Occult Tarot 1870–1970* (New York: St. Martin's, 2002).
Katz, Marcus, and Tali Goodwin, *Secrets of the Waite-Smith Tarot* (Woodbury, MN: Llewellyn, 2015).

1912: Carl Jung Breaks with Sigmund Freud
Hoeller, Stephan A., *The Gnostic Jung and the Seven Sermons to the Dead* (Wheaton, IL: Theosophical Publishing House, 1982).
Jung, Carl Gustav, *Memories, Dreams, Reflections*, ed. Aniela Jaffe (New York: Pantheon, 1962).

1913: Rudolf Steiner's Anthroposophical Society
Lachman, Gary, *Rudolf Steiner: An Introduction to His Life and Work* (New York: TarcherPerigee, 2007).
Steiner, Rudolf, *The New Essential Steiner* (Great Barrington, MA: Lindisfarne Books, 2009).

1917: The Thule Society
Goodrick-Clarke, Nicholas, *The Occult Roots of Nazism* (New York: New York University Press, 1992).

1921: Margaret Murray's *The Witch-Cult in Western Europe*
Murray, Margaret, *The Witch-Cult in Western Europe* (Oxford: Oxford University Press, 1921).
Oates, Caroline, and Juliette Wood, *A Coven of Scholars: Margaret Murray and Her Working Methods* (London: Folklore Society, 1998).

1922: Alfred Watkins Discovers the Leys
Pennick, Nigel, and Paul Devereaux, *Lines on the Landscape* (London: Robert Hale, 1989).
Watkins, Alfred, *The Old Straight Track* (London: Methuen, 1925).

1924: Harry Houdini Battles Fake Mediums
Jaher, David, *The Witch of Lime Street* (New York: Crown, 2015).
Keene, M. Lamar, *The Psychic Mafia* (Amherst, NY: Prometheus Press, 1997).

1925: The "Wars of the Roses"
Churton, Tobias, *The Invisible History of the Rosicrucians* (Rutland, VT: Inner Traditions, 2009).

McIntosh, Christopher, *The Rosicrucians: The History and Mythology of an Occult Order* (Wellingborough, UK: Aquarian, 1987).

1926: The Fulcanelli Enigma
Dubois, Geneviève, *Fulcanelli and the Alchemical Revival* (Rochester, VT: Destiny Books, 2006).
Fulcanelli, *Le mystère des cathédrales*, trans. Mary Sworder (London: Neville Spearman, 1971).

1928: Manly P. Hall's *The Secret Teachings of All Ages*
Hall, Manly Palmer, *The Secret Teachings of All Ages* (Los Angeles: PRS Press, 1988).
Sahagun, Louis, *Master of the Mysteries: The Life of Manly Palmer Hall* (Port Townsend, WA: Process Media, 2008).

1929: End of the Order of the Star in the East
Krishnamurti, Jiddu, *Think On These Things* (New York: HarperOne, 1989).
Vernon, Roland, *Star in the East: Krishnamurti—the Invention of a Messiah* (London: Palgrave Macmillan, 2001).

1935: Dion Fortune's *The Mystical Qabalah*
Fortune, Dion, *The Mystical Qabalah* (London: Rider, 1935).
Knight, Gareth, *Dion Fortune and the Inner Light* (Loughborough, England: Thoth, 2000).

1936: Dane Rudhyar's *The Astrology of Personality*
Ertan, Deniz, *Dane Rudhyar, His Music, Life, and Thought* (Rochester, NY: Rochester University Press, 2009).
Rudhyar, Dane, *The Astrology of Personality* (Garden City, NY: Doubleday, 1970).

1948: Raymond Palmer Founds *Fate Magazine*
Nadis, Fred, *The Man from Mars* (New York: TarcherPenguin, 2013).

1954: Gerald Gardner's *Witchcraft Today*
Gardner, Gerald, *Witchcraft Today* (London: Rider, 1954).
Hutton, Ronald, *The Triumph of the Moon* (Oxford, UK: Oxford University Press, 1999).

1960: The Modern Alchemical Revival
Albertus, Frater (Albert Reidel), *The Alchemist's Handbook* (New York: Weiser, 1960).

1969: John Michell's *The View Over Atlantis*
Michell, John, *The View Over Atlantis* (New York: Ballantine, 1972).

1979: Wicca Goes Mainstream
Adler, Margot, *Drawing Down the Moon* (Boston: Beacon Press, 1979).
Starhawk, *The Spiral Dance* (San Francisco: Harper, 1979).

1983: Ralph Blum's *The Book of Runes*
Blum, Ralph, *The Book of Runes* (New York: St. Martin's Press, 1978).

2012: The End of the Thirteenth Baktun
Argüelles, José, *The Mayan Factor: Path Beyond Technology* (Santa Fe, NM: Bear and Company, 1987).
Greer, John Michael, *Apocalypse Not* (San Francisco: Viva Editions, 2011).

INDEX

Note: Pages with illustrations appear in italics.

IMAGE CREDITS

ABOUT THE AUTHOR

John Michael Greer is one of the most widely respected writers and scholars in the occult field today. The author of more than forty books, including *The New Encyclopedia of the Occult*, he served for twelve years as Grand Archdruid of the Ancient Order of Druids in America (AODA). He lives in Cumberland, Maryland, with his wife, Sara.